HEIKE OWUSU

SYMBOLS
OF
AFRICA

Sterling Publishing Co., Inc.
New York

Library of Congress Cataloging-in-Publication Data Available

10　9　8　7　6　5　4　3　2

Published by Sterling Publishing Company, Inc.
387 Park Avenue South, New York, N.Y. 10016
First published in Germany under the title *Symbole Afrikas*
and © 1998 by Schirner Verlag
English translation © 2000 by Sterling Publishing Company, Inc.
Distributed in Canada by Sterling Publishing
c/o Canadian Manda Group, One Atlantic Avenue, Suite 105
Toronto, Ontario, Canada M6K 3E7
Distributed in Great Britain and Europe by Cassell PLC
Wellington House, 125 Strand, London WC2R 0BB, England
Distributed in Australia by Capricorn Link (Australia) Pty Ltd.
P.O. Box 6651, Baulkham Hills, Business Centre, NSW 2153, Australia

Sterling ISBN 0-8069-2871-9

About this book:

In this book, you will find over 300 symbols of sub-Saharan African peoples and tribes. To this day, a strongly expressive symbolism has been preserved in Africa, which shows itself in the ubiquitous ancestor worship, in art, and in daily life. These symbols range from ritual objects and masks, to the symbolic script of the Ashanti. They vary from utensils fraught with significance to ornaments and status symbols, all the way to the cave-paintings of the once fertile Sahara.

About the author & illustrator:

Early in her life, Heike Owusu had already acquired a spiritual view of the world. In her family and her social surroundings she encountered a lack of understanding for her spiritual interests. When a serious illness threatened her life, she conquered it with the help of autogenous training and a method of self-healing that she developed. Her great interest in the knowledge and mythology of the "natural peoples" was only strengthened through the marriage with her Ghanaian husband. All of this released her artistic potential, and thus today she relates her knowledge in various ways: through cosmic pictures, illustrations, and literary work.

TABLE OF CONTENTS

PREFACE

For Westerners, the African continent, with its rich symbolism, is still very difficult to understand. The over five and a half thousand tribes (which can be divided into several hundred language groups) all have their own rites, myths, and symbols. Africans, themselves, recognize only the meanings of the sculptures and signs of their own tribe. Many objects are unintelligible even for members of the tribe, if they are not members of one of the secret societies. Since, as part of magical ceremonies, many symbols are kept strictly secret, an exact interpretation is often very difficult to obtain or entirely impossible.

In sub-Saharan Africa, magic is still practiced everywhere and is often bound up with the custom of ancestor worship. Among some tribes-such as, for example, the Dogon (Mali)-all daily activities are subject to a strict rite and have a profound symbolic-religious meaning which derives from the tribe's own view of the world. Other ethnic groups, by contrast, have forgotten many of the connections of their cultural heritage because Western influence has fundamentally changed the structures of their communities.

In this book, I attempt to provide a comprehensive overview of the rich symbolism of this continent, a continent that is still shrouded in mystery. In order to be able to understand Africa, it is advisable to free oneself for a while from standardized Western thinking and to open oneself to other views of the world. Many ideals of beauty, ritual practices, and tribal marks are very difficult for Westerners to understand, yet they have their rightful place within a particular ethnic group.

In order to give the book a clearer organization, I divided Africa into six areas whose tribes display certain cultural similarities. Thus, we find that the ethnic groups in Western and Central Africa have countless representations by figures and a strongly developed mask worship. They were ruled (and sometimes still are) by powerful kings and influential secret societies. Some of these tribes have highly developed script like symbols.

The dark-skinned tribes of the Sahel zone and Northern Africa are for the most part culturally isolated, due to the sparse population and the difficult living conditions in this area. Their view of the world is often specific to the tribe, and ornaments and art objects are strongly stylized. In this area, the traditions are closely connected to Islam.

With the peoples of East Africa, on the other hand, we find hardly any sculptures or masks. In these mostly patriarchal communities, the manifold symbolism is found almost exclusively in clothing, ornaments, and hairdress. It corresponds to the pronounced sense of beauty of these tribes, who frequently spend all day decorating their bodies. This custom often stands in stark contrast to hard nomadic life and warlike temperament. It is likely that the nomadic way of life of the travelling herdsmen prevents the development of representations by figures, since these would only constitute superfluous ballast.

Unfortunately, due to strong Western influence, much of the cultural heritage of the southern part of the black continent has been lost. Therefore, the meaning of many objects is today no longer known. In this part of Africa, which is also a patriarchal society, masks are also hard to find. In addition, ornaments are used much more sparingly in this area. Communal life was (or is) characterized by two mutually opposed social forms: On the one hand, there are the leaderless groups such as the San or the !Kung* (Bushmen), on the other hand, we have old kingdoms such as that of the Zulu.

In general, one can say that the Africans approach their environment with great respect. They usually act carefully so as not to incur the wrath of spirits or ancestors. All beings, plants, and objects are regarded as "alive," that is, they are inhabited by a certain energy, for example, a spirit, which can be used by those knowledgeable in the art of healing and by sorcerers. The traditional view of the Africans is always a spiritual one in contrast with the rational, intellectually oriented view of the West.

Note: Except for some separately explained cases, the initiation ceremonies mentioned in the following texts always refer to rites which mark the transition from childhood to adulthood.

* The exclamation mark stands for the click, the peculiar characteristic of the language of the Bushmen.

ALL OF AFRICA

TRANSTRIBAL SYMBOLISM

Demon mask of the Senufo

DEMONS

In contrast with Judeo-Christian understanding, demons, according to the African view, are responsible for retributive justice. They are regarded as powerful spirits, who accord to everyone the lot that they deserve. Like most gods, demons too live in systems that are structured from the top down.

Every human being carries his or her own demon within, a demon who is at once identical with the person, yet the person's greatest enemy. This means that as individuals we must all deal with our destructive sides, with our fears, our anger, and our hatred. Whenever we yield to our negative side, we also feed the evil side of the demon, which can then easily gain the upper hand and escape our control. Hence, a positive person who knows him/herself well is not helplessly at the mercy of any demon. He or she might even get help from this being. There are well-meaning demons as well as evil ones.

Demons of the air were referred to as Djinns. Many phenomena, including dream experiences, were attributed to them. The friendly ones among them could be very beautiful, whereas the evil ones were easily recognized by their repulsive appearance. Stories speak of marriage-like unions between people and demons from which quite often children possessing special abilities are said to have originated.

The mask depicted here shows the demon Kponingo. It belongs to the mythical world of the Senufo in the Ivory Coast.

◆◆◆

Instrument of witchcraft with the beak of a hornbill

MAGICAL OBJECTs

The figure shows a typical instrument of witchcraft composed of a calabash (bottle gourd) and the head of a hornbill bird. In addition, cowrie shells have been attached on both sides. Even today, magical objects of this kind are used in Voodoo rituals in Africa and on the West Indian islands. They are made by medicine men or sorcerers. Here, the emphasis is not on the beauty of the instrument, but on the functional design. The more materials of power are bound together, the more effective the object will be. Parts of animals or plants always carry their energy and their special magical qualities.

It is impossible to assign the tools of witchcraft to certain groups, since they are usually adapted to the respective needs of the sorcerer who made them. The deeper meanings are also usually kept secret by the magicians. Only those initiated into the workings of witchcraft are able to understand the possible effects. Moreover, the objects are often filled with substances of magical power, which determine for what purpose the object will be used. Hence, the appearance of the object can give no clue to a black magic or white magic usage. Therefore, it is not necessarily the case that objects of a particularly frightening appearance serve an evil purpose or a harmful spell. Most tools of witchcraft in West Africa, for example, are not representations by figures but collections of various magical components. Some of them can be worn as charms; others are buried or kept in hidden places or altars.

Consequently, we can only speculate about the meaning of the object depicted above. In West Africa, the hornbill occupies the position of the highest town crier and is in a certain sense the king of the birds. Birds were responsible for transmitting news between the different dimensions and spheres. Cowrie shells, once the accepted currency of Africa, stood for wealth, power, and in some places for kingship. The calabash tied to the top probably served above all as a container of magical substances. Yet, it could also establish a connection to the feminine energies. In a magical ritual, the physical construction of the instrument was followed by the energetic charging or downright animation of the object.

1.

2.

3.

4.

FIGURINES FOR FERTILITY MAGIC

(1) Carved, wooden figurine, wrapped with strings of pearls. It is a cylinder doll of the Ambo tribe in Angola. It is supposed to represent a newborn child.

(2) Charm figurine of the Chokwe tribe, which invokes the spirit Cikunza. Cikunza promotes fertility and success in hunting. Women used to wear them on their belts. The spirit partook in initiation ceremonies in the form of a mask. Hunters would fasten the figurine to their hunting rifles and ask the spirit for a rich take.

(3) This figurine of the Bena Lulua in Zaire conveys the dual message of fertility and social status. The rich scar adornment, which in earlier times was very popular with the Lulua, indicates that this statuette belonged to a higher dignitary. It was part of the fertility cult of the Bwanga Bwa Chibola. The cult still exists today. The umbilical hernia of the figure is an indication of the dependence on the ancestors. Towards the bottom, the whole statuette is tapered to a point such that, for the purposes of the ritual, it could be stuck into the sand, thus creating a connection to mother earth.

(4) Fertility doll of the Ashanti, as it is still used today. The figurines are called Akuba, meaning "welcome." They are carved from the wood of a sacred tree and a worn on the neck or on the belt.

Sovereignty symbol of the chieftain's wife

◆◆

SPOON SCULPTURE

Generally, spoons were only brought out on special occasions and served, above all, as representational purposes, shown by the example with the carved head on the handle shows very well. Such large spoons-the one depicted here is about the size of a ladle-were usually signs of the dignity of a chieftain's wife.

The main task of a chieftain's wife consisted primarily in regulating the affairs of women in the village community. But it also happened that a woman was elected to be chief or that she took over the dignity of chieftain after the death of her spouse. These customs are in part still alive today. Since, in some tribes, it was impossible according to the laws that a woman would take over the entire leadership of a tribe, this problem was often already satisfied by the fact that the woman holding the office of chieftain wore men's clothing.

Such apparent contradictions have again and again made it difficult for Europeans to understand the more liberal African way of thinking.

Symbol of magical power

◆◆

Islamic Ornament

This sign comes from a miniature Koran of the Haussa people in northern Nigeria. It is the typical Islamic magic sign, as it can be found in all Muslim areas south of the Sahara. This is a characteristic symbol of the black, Islamicized population of Africa. It stands for the enormous magical power wielded by Islam.

Even the areas that had converted to Islam held fast to their old, heathen customs. Thus, Islam was never able completely to attain control over the darker skinned population. Everywhere, people simultaneously revered Islamic amulets and heathen fetishes, and they still do today. Non-Islamic peoples would also make use of Islamic prayers and healers in cases where their own medicine men failed.

The magical powers attributed to Muslims were generally met with awe and respect.

TRIBE-SPECIFIC IDEALS OF BEAUTY IN

1.

(1) AmaNdebele woman from South Africa with traditional neck ornaments. Today, however, these oranments are very rarely found amongst young women.

For the AmaNdebele, the woman with the longest neck was the most beautiful. From childhood on, more and more brass rings were added over the years until in this manner the neck was stretched to a length of 40 to 50 cm and more. The rings, of course, could never be removed since-for lack of neck muscles-this would have led to immediate death.

2.

(2) This figure shows a woman from the tribe of the Kichepo in eastern Sudan. For a long time, round or wedge-shaped lip disks have been an important means of beautifying the female body. Traditionally, this ornament was worn when men and mothers-in-law were present. The women tried to resemble certain birds, which have a ritual significance such as the spoon bill or the swamp courser.

Ornaments with protec- tive function

In some tribes, this custom probably also goes back to the deterring effect on slave traders. Nowadays, the younger generation only wears lip pegs or no lip ornaments at all.

22

3.

(3) Woman from the tribe of the Musgu wearing an upper lip peg made of aluminum. This form of mouth ornament was also common among other tribes of Chad. As children, the Lobi and Kirdi girls had their ears, lips, and noses pierced. The ornaments, to be worn later, served to protect these orifices, through which evil spirits with supernatural powers could easily have passed. The women of the Lobi and Kirdi tribes wore lip disks of up to 3 cm that were made from wood, clay, stone, or metal. The women of the Sara tribe wore upper lip pegs, which were the size of saucers and made speaking almost impossible.

4.

(4) The skull-stretching of the Mangbetu was performed until recently. It corresponded to the ideal of beauty of this tribe and was supposed to protect against witchcraft. A few days after birth, the head of the child was wrapped tightly. Later, a long cylindrical hair knot was often worn in order to increase the effect of the reshaping.

(5) An ear pin of the Fali women that was supposed to protect against the intrusion of evil spirits.

5.

23

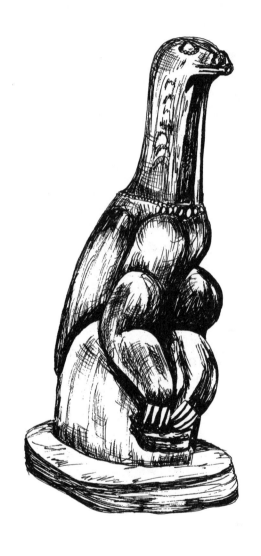

The eagle: mediator between worlds

◆◆

EAGLE STATUE OF THE SHONA TRIBE

This three foot bird sculpture made from soap stone was found together with seven similar objects in the ruins of Zimbabwe. It stood near the houses where the pregnant wives of the king were staying. The eagle is said to deliver news from the ancestors. By means of a good connection with his ancestors, the king was able to secure for himself and for the people wealth and good health. This was the most important spiritual task of the ruler. It was thought that the ancestors were speaking to God by influencing the climb of the eagle in a certain way.

The stone sculptures reflect the role of mediator, which the ruler occupied in the eyes of his subjects between God, the ancestors, and humans. Besides the typical features of the eagle, these sculptures also reveal some features of human beings. Thus, the bird depicted here has lips instead of a beak and ten fingers instead of the talons of the eagle. His sitting position indicates that he represents an important female official, probably the ritual sister of the king, the so-called "great aunt" of the kingdom.

The other seven sculptures that have been found depict standing eagles with human like features. They represent the ancestral spirits of the male leaders.

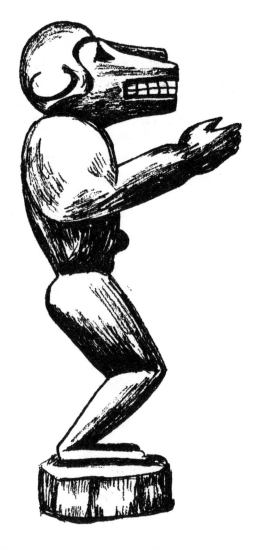

The ape: protector of the living

◆◆

APE

According to the general view, the apes keep the spirits of the deceased away from the villages of the living. The statue depicted in the drawing derives from the Baule, an Akan-speaking people on the Ivory Coast. It portrays the ape god Gbekre, who is a brother of the buffalo spirit Guli. Both are sons of the god of the heaven, Nyame. Gbekre is responsible for the punishment of the evil souls in the beyond. Since he is also revered as the god of the field, his image is often presented with offerings.

Chimpanzees occupy a special role among the apes. Because of their great likeness to humans, they are often regarded as beings mixed of apes and humans. In many myths, they are accorded human ancestors. Since they are regarded as protectors of humans, it is condemnable to kill them.

Gorillas, on the other hand, are regarded more as a human race of its own that lives deep in the jungle and, according to Ethiopian mythology, do not descend from Adam and Eve. Their size and power instill respect. In myths and stories, we frequently find reports of mixed marriages between humans and gorillas.

The buffalo: power & endurance

BUFFALO

The buffalo mask depicted here derives from the Dan (eastern Liberia and the western Ivory Coast). The mask is made of wood and decorated with two buffalo horns. In Africa, buffaloes are regarded as extremely powerful animals. Their strength, power, and endurance inspire respect in hunters, who can almost never succed in killing one of them. If a man displays features attributed to these animals, he is called a buffalo.

The mask serves to invoke the powers of the buffalo. In many parts of Africa, these animals were associated with the power of witches. Hence, they are also called upon to drive evil out of the community.

CHAMELEON

Chameleon: wisdom & caution

The object pictured here is a dance fixture of the Afo, a tribe related to the Yoruba of Nigeria. A chameleon moves carefully over razor-sharp points without getting hurt.

In Africa, the chameleon is generally associated with wisdom. In South Africa, it is called "work carefully" in Afrikaans and "Mr. Slow" in the Zulu language. According to a fable, after having created human beings, God sent the chameleon to earth in order to give them the message that, like the moon, every human being will come back to life after his or her death. Yet, because the chameleon was so slow, God also sent the hare with the same important message; but the hare ran away before he had properly heard the message. Everywhere, he now spread the news that all humans would have to die forever. The chameleon arrived too late, and the mistake could not be corrected. The moral of this story is, haste can lead to misfortune.

The chameleon also represents the ability of adapting to the changes of the world, since it can change its color. In Zaire, some tribes believe they are able to trace their lineage back to the white chameleon. Others regard the chameleon as a powerful god who is able to appear in different guises.

Elephant: size & power

ELEPHANT

In the traditional fables and myths, the elephant always embodies the wise chieftain, who attends to the needs of humans and animals. His character is considered to be magnanimous and compassionate. Many clans trace their origin back to an elephant and honor him as their totem. Other tribes report that the elephants were once humans. They had been transformed into animals either through witchcraft or through the influence of divine beings. These animals, moreover, which have no natural enemies, are also admired for their size and their strength. For they can only be conquered by humans and then only with the help of weapons and magic.

The Ashanti in Ghana see in an elephant a chieftain from their past. When they find such an animal dead in the woods, they arrange a burial ceremony on its behalf, as is done in honor of a chieftain. In many Ashanti proverbs, elephants are mentioned as well, as, for example: "The person who follows the path of an elephant does not get wet from the dew." This means that the person who follows an important man will be protected by him.

Fish: wealth & abundance

FISH

In their world view, the African peoples who fish often associate wealth and abundance with the species of fish from which they live. As symbols, these fish are then often reserved for the rulers. The drawing depicts a golden weight of the Ashanti, which represents a silurid. The silurid is commonly regarded as a subordinate to the crocodile. As such, he also appears in many proverbs. In general, fish are not regarded as mute in Africa. On the contrary, they are often said to have bewitching voices to which people again and again have fallen prey. Such fish are then usually regarded as embodiments of water spirits.

Frog: resurrection from the dead; bat: spirits of the deceased

◆◆

FROG

In the oldest African myths, the frog is often revered as a god and brought in direct association with the resurrection from the dead. Most tribes ascribe special magical powers to frogs, since these animals have the ability to bury themselves deep into the ground for many months during the dry season in order to await the beginning of the rainy season. Frogs have even been found which had been locked into rocks for several hundred years-and which were still alive. This relates to their ability to invoke the rain. And since these animals are said to able to come and go in the underworld, they are said to have a good connection to the god of the dead.

BAT

Widespread among the African peoples is the belief that bats are the spirits of the deceased which visit their relatives in this form. In South Africa, bats that stay around cemeteries are associated with spirits. These little spirits can either hurt humans, or they can help them in a treasure hunt if they are fed with blood.

The giant bats of Ghana are regarded as allies of sorcerers and gnomes (Mmoatia). Although the animals only feed on fruits, it is said that they abduct human beings and bring them to places to which evil spirits carry off their victims. Indeed, this species of bats does reveal a certain similarity with evil dwarfs: their feet point backwards, their hair is red, and moreover, they wear a beard.

left: Hare: cleverness; right: hen: care

HARE

This hare mask is attributed to the Dogon people in Mali. As a fable animal, the hare is very popular in Africa. It embodies the weak one who is superior to others because of his cleverness. A typical example is the tale in which a hare ends the tyranny of a lion. The hare tricked the lion into believing that his own mirror image in a well was a rival. The lion then plunged to his death.

In many places, the hare in the stories also takes on the role of the jester who has his fun with the larger animals and gets away unharmed. His weakness, however, is impatience and superficiality.

HEN AND ROOSTER

This gold-plated wooden parasol top is of Ashanti origin. It represents a hen with chicks. The fixture once sat atop one of the large parasols of an Ashanti ruler. The parasols could have a diameter of up to 4 meters. This symbol reminded people that a good king had to be benevolent tyrant, if he was to protect his people, and that he could become dangerous, if one opposed him.

Another expression says "The hen might kick her chicks, but that she will never kill them." Generally, here we are dealing with a symbol of harmlessness and care.

In the kingdom of Benin, a rooster cast in bronze was the special symbol of the queen mother.

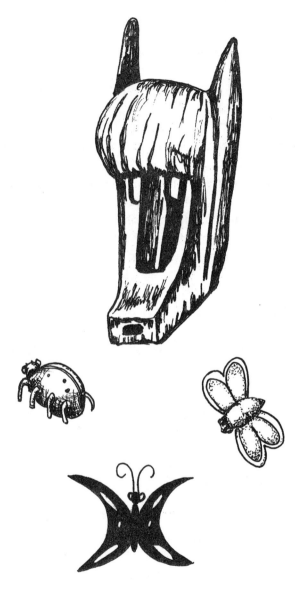

Hyena: ally of sorcerers; insects: cleverness, industriousness &
honesty

HYENA

In Africa, hyenas are regarded as allies of sorcerers and witches. Some tribes believe that witches use them as means of transportation. Others recount how sorcerers in the form of hyenas devour their victims and subsequently transform back into human beings. The people in Sudan know of evil sorcerers who set the predators on their enemies in order to kill them. In East Africa, many people claim to see the shining eyes of the dead, whom they have eaten, in the glowing eyes of the animals. In many places, it is also said that ancestors could ride on the hyenas by night to visit their living relatives. The drawing shows a hyena mask of the Ntomo alliance of the Bambara in Mali.

INSECTS

In Ghana, many fables deal with Anansi, the spider man. He is characterized as clever, industrious, and honest. In some parts of Central Africa, spiders are associated with the god Tule. He once descended to earth on a spider's thread in order to distribute the seeds of all the plants, which he had brought from heaven. And with the help of a magic drum, he got them all to germinate. According to the tradition, Tule could at any time show himself in human form.

In Africa, the fly is commonly referred to as dirty, for it likes to sit on excrements. In addition, it has the task of a spy, since it is easily able to enter into every room to eavesdrop and to observe.

Butterflies, according to the view of some tribes, can be carriers of the human soul.

Leopard: boldness

LEOPARD

The ivory sculpture of a leopard pictured here comes from Benin and was the property of the Oba (king). A coral necklace surrounding the abdomen of the animal pointed to the mystical kinship with the ruler who was also called the "leopard of the city." Ivory was used for the portrayal of the animal. The animal expressed the fact that the Oba took the characteristics of both the elephant and the leopard. According to a legend of the Edo, the elephant and the leopard once fought over supremacy in the jungle. Objects and masks with leopard representations were reserved for the king, as a symbol of his authority. He also kept living specimens of the wildcats in his palace.

Leopards occupy a special position in many African countries, one that is closely tied to ideas of magic. The kings of Zaire and South Africa laid claim to this emblem. The leopard enjoys great admiration for its fast and sure leap, which never misses its target. This makes the leopard a symbol of boldness and cunning. In many places we also find reports involving magical ideas where human beings take on the form of leopards.

Lion: charm, strength, and loyalty

LION

In the view of many African peoples, God takes on the form of a lion when he reveals himself to humans. Human flesh eating lions are often regarded as kings from ancient times who return to defend their empire. The spiritual power of a lion is so great that its mere presence can heal a person from severe illness. In addition, the lion possesses a powerful spell, which it can cast on an animal in order to kill it. For, without the will of the gods, no animal will die.

Many African rulers trace their origin back to lions. There are many stories, that tell of unions between lions and humans. Their progeny are mixed beings. Such half-lions usually have great magical abilities and may appear in human or in lion form. These creatures can become very dangerous to their human partners, since the hunting instinct if often stronger than love; yet in some stories, the loyalty of lions is emphasized as well. Many tribes report cases in which women have been seduced in the bush by lion-men and men have been seduced by lion-women. The animals are held to be very potent. A single hair from the eyebrow of a lion is supposed to give a woman the power to rule over a man by catching his spirit.

Hippopotamus: god mother;
Cattle: symbol of the life sustaining female principle

HIPPOPOTAMUS

In southern Mozambique, as in ancient Egypt, hippopotami were revered as goddesses. They are often referred to as the great mothers. Many tribes believe that underwater the hippopotamus rules over a wonderful green land in which colorful flowers bloom. The hippopotamus goddess is regarded as the protector of pregnant women and babies. In old stories, we are told that underwater, she takes care of many human infants. These are infants whom she has previously saved or who have been entrusted to her. In Mali, myths speak of a hippopotamus monster that terrorized people and ate their rice crops. Eventually, it was possible to conquer this powerful being, but only through the magic of a woman.

CATTLE

This box stored cola nuts. In Benin, cows played an important role as sacrificial animals. Cattle enjoy a special prestige in all of Africa. In the Sahel zone, the existence of many tribes depends on the state of their herds. In this area, cattle serve as currency and as dowries.

In the myths and legends of the pastoral tribes, they are often brought into a special relation with people. Thus, cows have always had a strong connection to women in their role as nurturers. For the ancient Egyptians, even the night sky was a cow, the goddess Nut. The animals are a symbol of the life sustaining female principle.

Bulls, on the other hand, have a strong and protective role, one which connects them spiritually with young men. They stand for the male principle that includes aggressiveness.

Turtle: intelligence & prudence; snake: teacher of the art of healing

◆◆

TURTLE

Because of its slow movements, the turtle is regarded as intelligent and prudent. Because it can reach old age, it is assured great respect; the repect that is paid to the elders of the tribe. This association is also strengthened by the wrinkly skin of these animals.

In legends, the wise turtle always comes away victorious. Since it is protected by its shell, no animal is able to kill it. The ability to carry its protective house is also interpreted as intelligence. Because turtles can live in water as well as on land, they are considered to be intimate friends of the god of rain and the water spirits.

SNAKE

This representation of a snake stems from the area of the Akan-speaking peoples (mainly Ghana). Snakes enjoy great admiration and respect in Africa. They are messengers of the ancestors or are regarded as spiritual beings. Thus, a Zulu king may reappear after his death as a giant Mamba. In many places, it is customary during a ritual for a snake to possess a participant. In this state, the snakes are then either asked to bring rain or a prophesy like an oracle. For many tribes, snakes embody water spirits. Among the Chokwe, pregnant women are believed to have a snake in their womb. It is an ancestral spirit, which supports the embryo in its growth and prepares it for life. Snakes are teachers of the art of healing and participate in the initiation ceremonies of future sorcerers and medicine men. Offerings are almost always brought to snakes.

Scorpion: power & insidiousness; porcupine: defensive power

SCORPION

The drawing shows a golden sculpture of an Ashanti king. Africans in general approach the scorpion with respect since some species are able to kill a person with their poison. The scorpion stands for power and sinister actions.

A saying of the Ashanti states: "The scorpion Kofi, son of God, does not bite with the mouth, but with the tail." This means that an enemy will not fight openly, but will try to harm his victim secretly. As insignia of the king, scorpions express the danger that the king poses to enemies.

PORCUPINE

Although they are relatively small inhabitants of the bush, porcupines are well able to defend themselves. According to stories, they employ their quills like firearms, which is why they are seldom pursued by hunters. In the symbolic world, they are mostly associated with military activities and soldiers. Among the Akan-speaking peoples (mainly Ghana), there exist several well-known proverbs, e.g.: "Ashanti warriors are like the quills of a porcupine-a thousand will grow again when a thousand have fallen." Or: "Who would dare attack a porcupine which is protected by so many quills?"

Since the animals show little aggressiveness and use their quills only when attacked, they are commonly associated with the power of defense.

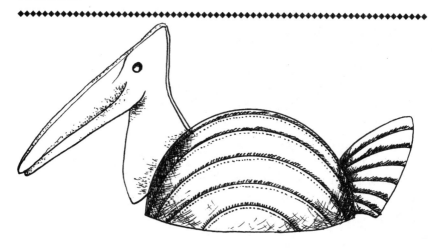

Birds: carriers of the souls

BIRDS

The illustration shows a soul bird in the form of a dance fixture. In all African ethnic groups, the soul is considered immortal, and, like body and mind, it is regarded as an objective substance. Evil sorcerers, who have already made a considerable number of enemies through their deeds, hide their soul substance in a box. This box is hidden within several other boxes, which in turn are inserted into the body of a living animal, preferably a bird. If this bird dies, the life of the sorcerer is ended as well. In all African cultures, birds are associated with souls. In many places, it is thought that the soul of a person who has died because of black magic can fly about in the form of a songbird.

about in the form of a songbird.

In Zimbabwe, swallows are considered to be related to the sun birds. They are admired as the fastest and most skilled flyers. Like the sunlight, they are able to traverse a dark space without being caught. According to legend, the first day broke when the two sun birds were caught.

In East Africa, pigeons are a symbol of reciprocal love. They stay faithful to each other for a lifetime. With the Yoruba in Nigeria, they are ritual sacrificial animals, which symbolize honor and wealth.

In Africa, as elsewhere, owls are the birds associated with witches. Witches either work together with the animals or can even assume their form. In Malawi, owls are consulted in the context of an oracle. In many places, however, the cry of an owl is seen as a bad omen.

In Zaire, the falcon is considered the bearer of light. After the falcon was freed from imprisonment in the underworld, it rose into the sky and let the sun rise with it.

Many tribes revere the wisdom of the vulture, who is able to gain life from death. They are often also referred to as soul birds since some East African peoples believe that vultures carry within them the souls of the bodies they have consumed. Hence, they are also seen as deliverers of offerings to the gods. Without the vultures, no offering can be successfully carried out.

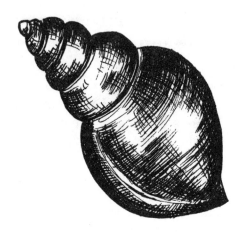

Water snail: creator of the river; ram: masculinity & thunder

WATER SNAIL

Akan-speaking peoples belive that the water snail was originally a golden weight who was transformed by the Gods. According to legend, the snail Apupuo Yaa created the river, yet is prohibited from using it. Water snails are commonly regarded as dirty animals and appear as such in many proverbs.

RAM

Outside of the highlands of Kenya, sheep are seldom found in Africa. For the Berbers in Morocco and Berber speaking people in southwestern Egypt, the ram is associated with the sun. The Swahili celebrate their New Year's Day on March 21, when the sun enters the sign of Aries; this day is called Nairuzi-the similarity to the Farsi word Nau Ruz, which means "new light," is unmistakable. In Persia, the ram was once revered as an embodiment of the god of light. Hottentots in Namibia have stories of the sun ramas well. They call it Sore-Gus. Other tribes, such as, for example, the Akan-speaking peoples of West Africa, associate the ram with masculinity and thunder. All share the idea that the ram always embodies a masculineactive, partly also aggressive power.

The drawing represents a ram mask from Cameroon.

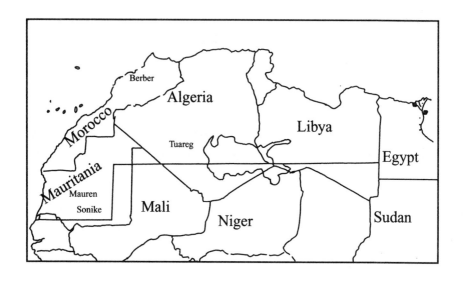

THE NORTH

NORTH AFRICA & SAHEL ZONE

MOROCCO

ALGERIA

LIBYA

EGYPT

MAURITANIA

MAURITANIA

MALI

NIGER

CHAD

SUDAN

UPPER VOLTA

NIGERIA

Wodaabe Dancer on the annual marriage market

BEAUTY TRAITS AMONG THE WODAABE

The Wodaabe, who inhabit parts of Niger, Nigeria, and Cameroon in nomadic groups, gather annually for the Jereol festival, and subsequently, weddings and naming festivals. During these festivals, which all take place during the rainy season, ornaments play an important role. In daily life, the Wodaabe limit themselves to wearing magical charms. Newborns already receive leather pendants, the boys for the development of masculinity, the girls for the promotion of fertility.

Beauty is of highest importance to the Wodaabe who consider themselves to be the most beautiful people on earth. In order to ensure that a wife will bear beautiful children, her husband, in case he is not attractive enough, will let her sleep with other men.

The prestige of a man depends on the size of his herd of animals. Status symbols of the women are artistic decorative calabashes which have no practical value and which are carried along through the bush on the back of an ox.

(1) This figure shows a young man at a Jereol festival. The face painting is supposed to emphasize the elongated shape of the face and the narrow nose. In order to increase the seductive power of the dancer, a ritually produced paste from yellow powder is applied to the face. The dots on the cheekbones, however, are pure decoration. A black ostrich feather on the head serves to increase the masculinity. During the trance-like dance, lasting several hours, the dancers attempt to attract young girls by means of lustful looks and wild faces.

Balancing on the tips of their toes, they try to display their

Wodaabe maiden in festival dress

charisma and charm. Among the Wodaabe, beauty means white eyes, a long narrow nose, white and even teeth, and a slim, tall body. At the end of the dance, every girl chooses the man she likes best and spends the night with him.

(2) The girl in this drawing is a judge and a spectator at the Jereol festival. The long thin braids in brass tubes signal that this girl is considered to be especially beautiful.

Until the birth of their first child, young women wear heavy leg rings, which they receive as presents from their mothers. The weight of these rings lends the gait of the girls a seductive sway. The number of ring pairs reveals the wealth of the girl. The facial tattoos protect against the evil eye.

Veil as sign of social rank (Tuareg)

TUAREG VEIL

In the nomadic society of the Tuareg, only the men veil themselves, while the women openly display their face and hair. The number of veils and the manner of wearing them gives information about the man's social status. The Tagelmoust consists of a strip of cloth six yards long. Beginning with puberty, the Tuareg man veils himself, thus protecting him from sand, wind, and heat in the desert. Even in the camp and while drinking, he does not remove the veil, so that no one may see his mouth. Indigo blue dye is difficult and expensive to obtain in the desert. Dark blue veils, which are given a metallic effect by beating them dry, are worn only by rich men.

The higher his social rank, the more a man will try to hide his face, often leaving only a small slit for the eyes. Some men wear cloth amulets, like the one in the drawing. Special objects of prestige which signal a high social position are the small amulet boxes (Cherots) made from silver, brass, or copper that are worn on the head (see figure).

SYMBOLISM OF THE TUAREG OR-NAMENTS

(1) At the age of 17, every girl receives from her mother the Khommissar pendant in the form of a stylized hand together with a Cherot. The one shown here comes from the Niger Tuareg who live in Mali. It is above all meant to ward off the evil eye. In addition, it is made from shells in order to promote fertility.

(2) This Cherot comes from the women of the Kel-Ahaggar Tuareg. Such amulet boxes are worn in different varieties in all tribes of the Tuareg by men as well as by women. Pieces of paper with verses from the Koran or magic charms by the holy man Marabou are kept in them. The box-usually made from silver-is worn daily by its owner as a talisman.

(3) Tuareg crosses are considered to be powerful good luck charms and are also very popular in other tribes. They are usually made from silver, a highly valued metal among the Tuareg. Gold, on the other hand, is avoided as a material that brings bad luck. The names of the crosses most often refer to oasis towns. The In-Waggeur cross, shown here, is a fertility symbol for both men and women. The circle stands for the female principle; the phallic

60

motif stands for the male principle.

(4) Originally, Tuareg crosses were ornaments for men. In puberty, the son received them from his father along with the words: "I give you the four corners of the world because one never knows where one will die." The number four is thus found in all crosses as a symbol of the four directions. The Aagades cross, seen here, also features engravings of the eye of a chameleon and the tracks of a jackal. Both are signs of strength and cunning.

(5) The Tanfouk, which consists entirely of carnelian, is an old symbol of good luck and protection. It is worn by all Tuareg groups in combination with other neck crosses. Like other ornaments made from carnelian, it is also supposed to promote the healing of wounds.

(6) The girls of the Ullimeden Tuareg like to wear delicate necklaces with silver pendants. In the middle, one often finds such a pendant in the shape of a triangle which as a good eye is supposed to ward off the evil eye. The triangle also stands for female fertility.

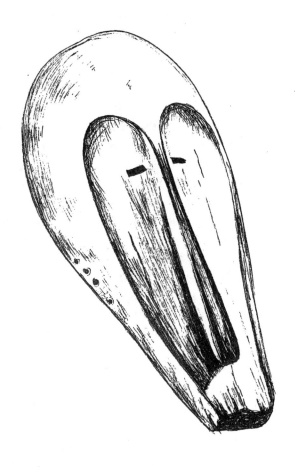

Mask of a secret society that ensures law and order (Fang)

◆◆◆

FANG MASK

These white masks of strict geometrical form come from the Fang, also called Pangwe or Pahouin, who live in southern Cameroon, Gabon, and Equatorial Guinea. These masks belong to the attributes of the secret society Ngil, which had the task of ensuring that law and order were upheld. The Fang were a patriarchally oriented society. Men who wanted to join the society had to undergo an arduous and bloody initiation ritual. The Ngil masters guarded the peace between the clans and enemy villages. Accompanied by their entourage, they moved from place to place to administer justice and render judgments. The masks heightened their dramatic appearance. In combination with a fringe ruff and a costume made from raffia palm fibers, they evoked the impression of a terrifying half-human being. During the nightly appearances, this effect was strengthened by the flickering light of torches.

The white color of the masks symbolizes their relation to the spirits. Often, it was the task of the secret society to convict and condemn sorcerers. Shady dealings and evil magic were punished with the death penalty.

Anthropomorphic representation of the sun

◆◆◆

SUN

The figure to the side shows a bronze pendant from Upper Volta of a sun with human facial features. In contrast with Egypt, sun worship is not very widespread in black Africa. Yet, among many peoples we find myths about an era of darkness, which was overcome through the discovery of the sun. Moreover, the Swahili word Jua, Iruva, or Lyuba, which means God, also means sun in various central African languages. Presumably, the old sun rituals have been forgotten and exist only in stunted form in some tribes. The Duala, for example, pray to the sun god Loba after sunset, and the Jagga in Tanzania greet the rising sun with a prayer. Among the Bantu, remnants of this cult can be observed. In Nigeria, the Yoruba, who call themselves Omo Orun or children of the sun, revere the sun god Orun. Offerings are still presented to him, but even his worship is on the wane.

Sun worship is primarily found in patriarchally organized societies, since the sun itself is regarded as male. In the imagination of some tribes, the sun lives with his wife in a bright palace, where he rests at night from his daily work. The sun brings the light into the darkness and nurtures life. It is generally ascribed great healing powers. The animals associated with it are the falcon and the ram (see also: Animals).

Earth spirit mask of the Mossi, Upper Volta

BOARD MASK

In Upper Volta, there lives a people by the name of Mossi who are both patriarchally organized and Muslim. Since the Islamic faith prohibits portrait representations, the mask faces are strongly reduced to essentials. The attached board features the X-pattern typical for the area. The spirit face of the mask reveals both human as well as animal traits. Masks like these were used by the Wango men's league on various ritual occasions. Thus, they served mainly as protection during burials in which women in Islamic societies may generally not be present. Hence, women were not allowed to see the masks. The masks are all considered to be the property of the earth spirit.

As in many African ethnic groups, here too, the fusion of the old natural religion and a foreign religion such as Islam becomes apparent. The deities of both systems of faith are revered equally.

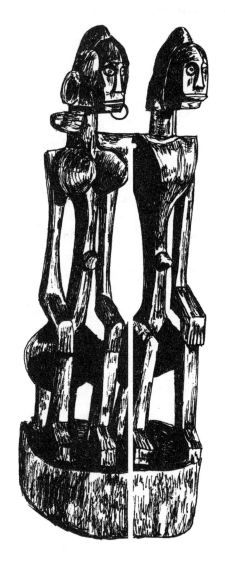

Ancestral couple of the Dogon, Mali

ANCESTRAL COUPLE OF THE DOGON

According to legend, the primordial parents of the Dogon were formed of clay by the divine creator Amma. After Amma had breathed life into his creatures, he circumcised them. Subsequently, the foreskin of the man transformed into a black and into a white lizard, while the clitoris of the woman turned into a scorpion. After the couple had united, the woman in succession gave birth to four pairs of twins. First, four boys were born, then four girls. The Dogon people trace their origin back to these eight ancestors.

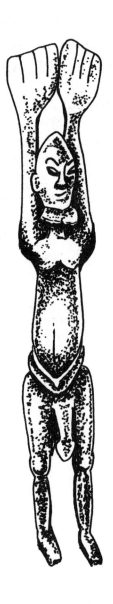

Creator-god of the Dogon, Mali

◆◆◆

AMMA

This figure, which is neither clearly male nor clearly female, represents the creator-god of the Dogon. According to myth, Amma first created the sun from an earthen pot, which he/she baked for a long time until it started to glow. Then, she/he entwined it eight times with a red copper spiral. Subsequently, she/he formed the moon following a similar principle. He/she created it a little bit smaller and wound a spiral of white copper (brass) around it. With the help of the sunlight, the shiny black people later emerged, while the white people were created in the moonlight.

Amma formed the earth from clay and gave it the shape of a woman lying with the head to the North and with the feet to the South. After he had mated with it, she gave birth to the golden jackal. The first animal was born. After a second mating between Amma and the earth, this time through the rain, a twin creature was born. It was a mixed being with a human body, green snake tails, and split tongues. This creature, by the name of Nummo, clothed Mother Earth with plants of all kinds. The wind caused by the movement of the twins was the first language on earth.

Later, Amma took some parts of the sun and distributed them in the sky; this is the origin of the stars.

Highly simplified human figure (Dogon, Mali)

HUMAN FIGURE WITH BOW

Like the Senufo, the Mande, and the Bambara, the ethnic group of the Dogon belongs to the Vota family of peoples. They all developed highly stylized forms of representation. Among the Dogon people, even the most basic utensils, engravings, and drawings have profound cosmic significance.

This characteristic figure represents a person holding a bow. The figure is reduced to a minimum, strictly linear, but full of life. It is an allusion to the original way of life of the Dogon. They were once hunters on the vast plateau before settling in the steep rock faces. According to the mythology, they drove another people away from there in the 15th century. To this day, they live in this natural fortification as sedentary farmers. They learned the art of weaving and of smithery. The end result is an expression of their rich view of the world. The blacksmith is regarded as the one who brought civilization. This is why his house is located at the northern end of the main square of the village. This, in turn, represents the first cultivated field of the Dogon. The blacksmiths trace their origin back to one of the eight ancestors of the Dogon, and they belong to a certain caste. To this day, they form iron figures such as the staff displayed here.

Heroic figure of the Bambara, Mali

◆◆

TYI WARA DANCE FIXTURE

Among the Mende peoples, in this case the Bambara in Mali, animal symbols are often employed for the purposes of illustrating human behavior. Dance fixtures like these in the shape of antelopes are found very frequently in this region. Tyi Wara means "animal of agriculture" and designates the mythical hero of the Bambara, who was half animal, half human. He taught them how to cultivate fields. Traditionally, he is represented as an antelope, although other forms exist as well. Sometimes, his appearance is mixed with the characteristic features of aardvarks or ant-eaters. Antelopes are regarded as graceful, aardvarks as conscientious and determined-values which are important in farming. If a successful farmer is compared to a courageous animal that survives in the wilderness, then he is being given the highest praise.

In the beginning, Tyi Wara was a male initiation society, which taught its members the art of agriculture and conducted secret dances in the fields. These mask dances were supposed to ensure the continuing favor of the antelope man. Later, dance fixtures like the one pictured here were carved and men and women started dancing together in pairs. Gradually, the once secret society became accessible to everyone.

Symbol of rebirth (Mali)

◆◆◆

MARIONETTE OF THE BAMBARA

This puppet was primarily used in the fertility rituals and not entertainment. It symbolizes the cycle of the rebirth of a living being. This is why all three faces reveal similarities and yet also individual traits. In the representation of the antelope, the Bambara honor Tyi Wara, a legendary hero who once taught them to cultivate the land. He was a mixture of human and antelope.

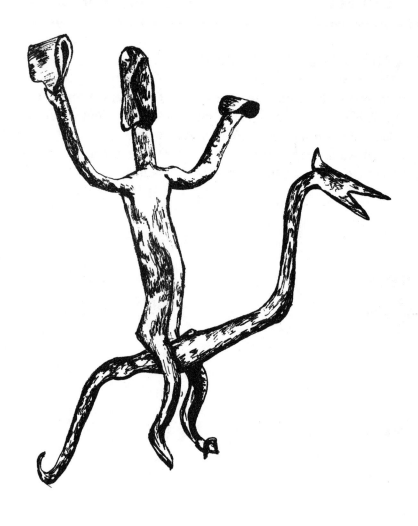

Symbol of magical power (Mali)

RIDER

This cast-iron figure comes from the Bambara. Like the Dogon, this people too has developed a highly simplified form of representation. The sculpture shows a human figure riding on a mythological monster.

As with many figures of the Bambara, here too the meaning does not seem to be clearly fixed. Symbolically, this object stands for the unification of human intelligence with the animal strength and magical power of a mythical being. This multiplies the strength of animal and rider. Only an intellectually and spiritually strong person is able to steer and control such a being and thus able to attain great power with its help.

Symbols of creation (Mali)

ASSEMBLY HOUSE OF THE DOGON

In the course of time, the Dogon people have developed an extraordinarily complex symbolism of everyday life, to an extent that is seldom found in African cultures. The prescriptions reach into the most intimate areas of family life. The assembly house of the men is represented here and is richly decorated with symbols. One of the most important motifs of the Dogon is the pair of twins. It is used to explain pairs of opposites such as male-female. Even the houses are usually arranged in twin form. As a rule, a village tucked into a rock face also has a twin village further down in the valley, which is set up in exactly the same form. The lizard on one of the supporting pillars symbolizes the male principle, while the breasts stand for the female principle.

The reed roof is three meters thick. It is supported by a total of eight pillars, which embody the eight ancestors of the Dogon. These mythical beings lived for a time as humans and were subsequently transformed into water spirits. If one follows the arrangement of these supporting pillars, one recognizes the image of a snake: it was the twin spirit Nummo, half human, half snake, who created the ancestors and brought the human race onto the earth. For his part, Nummo sprung from the union of the creator god Amma and the female Earth.

Wooden writing board of the Koran schools (Haussa, Sahel zone)

WRITING BOARD

Boards of this kind were used in the land of the Haussa in the classes of the Koran schools. The Haussa, a people of farmers and artisans, live in northern Nigeria, in Chad, in Niger, and in Upper Volta. The majority of the population has been Muslim since the 14th century.

The writing board depicted here was given to a student who had successfully graduated from the Koran school. On this occasion, the words "Allah sabka da Zayyana," which evoke the omnipresence of Allah, were written on the board and would never be erased. The graphical ornamentation on this object of a size of 50 cm is typical of Islamic art in non Arabic parts of Africa.

Representation of birth

ROCK DRAWING

This rock drawing is from the Tassili mountains, a high plateau in the Sahara desert. Today it is uninhabitable. 6000 years ago, however, this region was populated by herdsmen and hunters. Numerous cave paintings show the existence of rich animal and plant life. While animals are often depicted very precisely, people, are usually shown in simplified motifs. The scene depicted in this rock drawing shows the event of a birth.

In the old matriarchal societies, the birth of a boy was usually not given much attention, while the arrival of a girl was celebrated at length.

In Africa, it is common to call upon the ancestors to welcome the newly arrived who will continue their lineage. This was preceded by various rituals of cleansing, washing, sacrifice, and pouring of drink offerings for ancestors. In the predominant view, ancestors could be reborn in one of their descendants. According to the common belief, the child received the blood of the mother and hence its status and its membership within the tribe. From the father, the child inherited the factors determining character, and from the highest god, it would receive its immortal soul.

Among the various tribes, the childbed lasted between 10 to 40 days. In some tribes, it was customary for the woman to get up right away and for the father to take her place in the childbed so as to deceive the evil spirits. The father would then undergo all the magical rites normally intended for the mother.

In other areas, mothers would dress in bright gowns after the birth and wear white pearls around the neck and the arms.

A priestess charming a red deer

ROCK DRAWING

For centuries, women were at the center of numerous sanctuaries. They fulfilled important tasks in magical procedures and in the practice of oracles. This rock drawing from the Tassili mountains shows a woman who is charming a red deer.

Priestesses originally worked in central sanctuaries, which in the old travel reports of the first European traders and explorers were compared to temples. They were also active in the "houses of the ancestors" and in the ritual sites of the community. Elaborately designed temples, decorated with life-size statues of people, animals, and deities, were built mainly in West Africa. Priestesses worked in such buildings as fortune-tellers, interpreters of oracles, and healing experts. These places had schools attached in which the priestesses would teach children, among other things, song and dance.

In West Africa, primarily in Ghana, such islands of matriarchy have been preserved until this day.

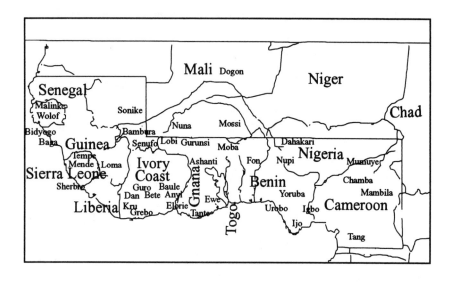

THE WEST

MALI
CHAD
SENEGAL
GUINEA
SIERRA LEONE
LIBERIA
IVORY COAST
GHANA
TOGO
BENIN
NIGERIA
CAMEROON

Magical figurines

MAGICAL FIGURINES

Wooden statues, such as these, are still frequently used by sorcerers for magical rituals. As is the case with a fetish, such a figurine is animated with a spirit. Usually, it is one of the servant spirits of the sorcerer who is forced by the master to enter into the sculpture and remain within it. Such figures can then be sent out to attack a certain victim without the identity of the sorcerer being revealed. These statues are not always used to harm others. They are also employed in acts of healing. Most often, however, the sorcerer has the goal of manipulating his environment with his acts. For his services, he often demands payment from his clients.

People quite frequently avail themselves of the help of sorcerers for purposes of defense, healing a close friend or relative, or, as is too often the case, in order to harm another person out of sheer envy.

(1) This figurine represents a natural spirit conceived in a human-like way. It comes from Cameroon and has the considerable height of 155 cm. According to the view of all African tribes, natural spirits live in the forests and animate the environment. They are usually to be feared.

(2) Here we see a female magical figure of the Bakongo from the area of the lower Congo. It is a container locked with glass in which magical substances and objects are kept. These can be either plants or parts of living or dead people.

(3) This magical figurine is made of wood and set with human teeth. It comes from Batanga in Zaire and stands 38 cm tall.

Magic utensil

MOTHER AND CHILD REPRESENTATION OF THE YORUBA

It was possible to increase the magical qualities of a utensil by means of an image of the primordial mother. Images of women were especially suitable for ritual purposes, since women were credited with a higher morality. This bowl, which is carried by a wooden sculpture, served to store cola nuts with the help of which the Ifa oracle was consulted. (see also: utensils of the Ifa oracle)

Mother and child representations reflect the hidden power of women, since they do not carry any weapons as insignia of power. Women give birth. That is to say, they give and they take at the same time, an act that is equivalent to an offering. Without this power of the mothers, kings would not be able to rule.

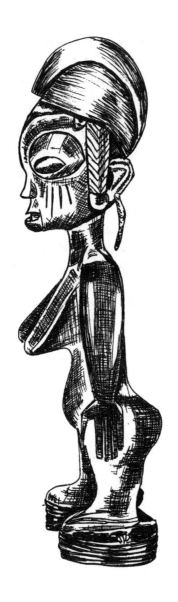

Twin deity from Nigeria

THE FIGURE IBEJI

For the Yoruba in Nigeria, Ibeji is the deity of the twins. There, people are convinced that the common soul of a pair of twins is indivisible. If for some reason, one of the twins should die, the mother will order two figures from an artist. According to the belief of the Yoruba, the deceased child will live on in one of these wooden figures and will thus share in the life of the other twin. Like a living child, this figure can then also be washed, fed, dressed, oiled etc.

The figurine represented here has a height of approximately 30 cm.

Magic figure of a rider (Ivory Coast)

◆◆◆

HUNTING FETISH

This sculpture of a female rider comes from the village of Latka on the Ivory Coast. It was carved from a piece of wood and its surface was blackened. The figure is approximately 40 cm tall. The figure served as a hunting fetish and was supposed to bring the hunters luck. Traditionally, hunters have always enjoyed a high standing in Africa. Before the hunt, dances and rituals were performed. Taboos were observed. Hunters bathed, rubbed their bodies with magical oils, practiced sexual abstinence, and avoided of certain foods. In some tribes, the spirits of the ancestors were implored to let the game out of the stables. In other tribes, the hunters had to ask the god of the game for permission in a certain way.

After a successful hunt when the hunters return to their villages, they are, even nowadays, celebrated by the women; and in some places it is customary that they sleep with the hunters if the hunters are bringing game. Generally, a fetish is an object that is inhabited by a spirit. The one shown here was charged by a sorcerer or a medicine man with the spirit of a female ancestor or a goddess. Like a silent servant, this spirit would then carry out the instructions of its owner.

THE PRIMORDIAL MOTHER

In West Africa, the primordial mother is traditionally represented as a large breasted figure sitting on a stool. Asking the goddess for a bountiful harvest and many children, the participants of a consecration ceremony would rhythmically tap the ground during a nocturnal procession.

In earlier times, mother goddesses were worshipped in all African areas south of the Sahara. Almost everywhere, the ideas that people have of her and the forms in which they represent her reveal great similarities. Most tribes see her as a powerful woman with large breasts with which she feeds her many children.

Only the myths and stories associated with the goddess differ from tribe to tribe. The Ewe in Togo say that before birth the soul of a child must visit a land called Amedzofe, the place of human genesis.

There, high in the mountains of

Sculpture of the earth goddess

central Togo, lives the spirit mother who teaches good manners to every child that is to be born on earth.

The Dogon in Mali trace their ancestry back to the god of the heavens, who once slept with the earth goddess. She, in turn, gave birth to twins.

In the Yoruba land in Nigeria, the earth goddess, Oduduwa, is still revered today. Her name means, "The ruler who, consisting of herself, created all living beings." The goddess herself must be regarded as the primordial material of the earth. Together with her spouse, the important god Obatala, she created the earth and all living beings.

The earth goddess Muso Kuroni, who is revered by the Bambara in Mali, has a rather wild and unpredictable side, similar to the Indian goddess of the forest, Kali-Parvati. Having once been with the sun god Pemba-who, assuming the shape of a tree, entered her with his roots-she gave birth to all the animals, plants, and human beings. The description of her appearance varies. Among other things, she is also seen as a black leopard, since she is also the goddess of darkness. As such, she attacks unsuspecting people, causes women to menstruate, and circumcises boys and girls who are to be humanized by this procedure and liberated from their savage state.

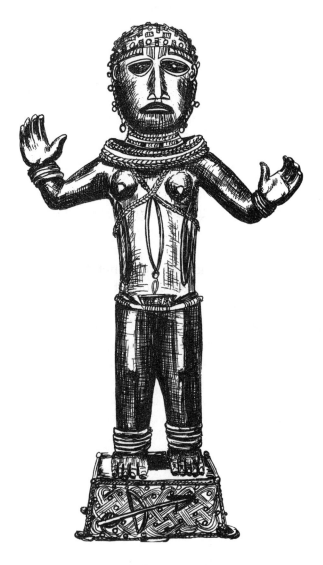

Statue of a Princess, Benin

PRINCESS IDEALLY

The statue of the princess was made in Benin, Nigeria, from brass and measures almost half a meter. Rich decorations on the pedestal in the form of ornately intertwined ribbons immediately identify the person represented as a high dignitary. Throughout Africa, such patterns were exclusively reserved for the royal families or high officials.

The symbol of the bow and arrow can be a reference to one of two things. First of all, it could illustrate that the princess was the head of a regiment of Amazons, which played an important role in Benin all the way into the 19th century. Or, secondly, it could mean that she herself possessed great skill in handling this weapon. Female warriors and palace guards were often found in the matriarchal societies of West Africa. In terms of skill and strength, they were in no way inferior to the male warriors.

The scant clothing of the princess shown here is an indication that she is still unmarried. Married women were in the habit of covering body and breasts.

The scar tattoos on the forehead, stomach, and sides are indications of her tribe and social position. Princesses generally enjoyed many privileges. A princess could choose any man from among the people as her spouse. She could then force him not to have any other woman besides her. And no man was allowed to refuse her wishes. It also happened that a princess married several men, as was also customary among queens. Like any other woman, she too had the right to dissolve a marriage at any time and to appoint a new man as her spouse.

Sculpture of unknown origin for ancestral and fertility rituals,
Sierra Leone

MAHANYATE SOAPSTONE HEAD

Soapstone heads of this kind come from Sierra Leone and Central Guinea. They are called Mahanyate and play an important role in the fertility rites of the Mende and Kru tribes. It is quite safe to say, however, that these ethnic groups are not the creators of these heads and sculptures. To this day, the current population finds such objects buried in the ground or in riverbeds. They probably come from the ancestors of today's Kissi, from an era prior to the 15th century. They all have protruding eyes, full lips, and a fleshy nose. The size of the figures ranges from 7 cm to life-size heads. Today, the Mende people believe that the stone heads were made by spirits. They refer to them as "gods of rice" and bring them offerings for a good harvest. The Kissi, on the other hand, believe that these are revelations of their ancestors, and they worship them at the ancestral altars.

Ritual figure for burials of the Poro alliances, Ivory Coast

RITUAL PESTLE

In former times, these figures were used in Mali as well as among the Poro alliances of men on the Ivory Coast, the counterparts of the Sande alliances of women. Originally, they were carved in pairs, as god and goddess.

The sculpture of a mother goddess shown here was created by a carver from the tribe of the Senufo. It is attributed to one of the sacred groves of the village of Lataha, to the so-called "white forest" (Kofile). The base of the pestle has probably broken off. These sculptures were normally used in rituals before and after the burial of a Poro elder. First, a novice carried them into the house of the deceased. From there, the statue accompanied the dead to the grave. At the grave site, it was tapped on the ground to the rhythm of the funeral music. When finally at dusk the grave had been covered with soil, a male novice jumped onto the grave mound in order to stamp down the ground with one of the pestles. This was supposed to ensure that the deceased really did leave on his journey to the "village of the dead" and did not remain in proximity to the living. The pestles might still be used in some rituals.

In Lataha, the pestle is called Ponno Shon, that is, Poro man. The concept, Denge or Madengo, which means bush spirit, is also known as a term for the pestle.

The highest judge of the world of the gods (Benin)

THE GOD GO

This life-size figure of the god Go, made of hammered brass, comes from the altar of the royal palace in Dahomey. The two ceremonial swords in his hands show his power and authority. For the Fon people, who inhabited Dahomey until the end of the last century, Go had the power over life and death.

In the state of Dahomey, which was ruled centrally and with military severity from the royal capital and in which annually human sacrifices were made, the god Go occupied one of the most important places in the world of the gods. The Fon people were feared by their neighboring tribes, since their male and female soldiers surpassed the others in wildness and skill.

Deity of the thunder storms from Nigeria

◆◆

THE GOD SANGO

Sango is traditionally represented with a double axe on the head. The axe describes the thunder bolt which the god of thunder and lightening hurls from the sky. The ritual staff shown here was carved by a priest of the Oshe Sango cult from the Yoruba land. It was used in religious ceremonies in order to prevent excessive rainfall. While rainmakers were needed in northern Nigeria, the southwestern part often suffered from too much rain. With the help of this magic wand, it was possible for the priests to control the amount of precipitation.

During the initiation rites, the novice got a polished stone axe tied on his head in order to demonstrate the unification of the human with the superhuman.

In many villages, one finds sacred shrines of Sango. In these shrines, the god is often represented with his three wives. Oya, Oshun, and Oba are likewise represented with a double axe or with ram horns on their heads. In spite of his violent temper, Sango is also regarded as the god of justice and decency. He punishes sinners by having them struck down by lightening. For this reason, people who are killed by lightening are despised. The Sango priests simply carry the body into the forest and leave it there.

*Symbols of the female and the male principle among the Yoruba,
Nigeria*

RITUAL STAFFS OF THE OGBONI ALLIANCE

This pair of sculptures was used by the Ogboni secret society of the Yoruba tribe for conjurations and ritual healings. It is typical of these ritual instruments that a male and a female figure are tied to each other with a chain. The male figure is seen on the left holding the reproduction of an Edan-Ogboni (scepter) in his hands. The female figure presents the secret and sacred greeting by putting the left fist over the right one while hiding her thumbs.

Such pairs of figures are cast at the occasion of the initiation of a member. For the Yoruba, they symbolize the omnipotence of the Ogboni alliance. The figures represent the founding couple of the alliance and stand at the same time for all the men and women of the Yoruba people. Generally, the sexual characteristics are especially worked out in these figures in order to draw attention to the significance of the duality. The Ogboni used to perform the more important rituals naked, since nudity, in the eyes of the alliance, allowed for more powerful magic. Even today, all guests and members of this society must bare their feet, chest or shoulders when entering the community center in order to demonstrate honesty, openness, and respect.

The large, slanted eyes of the two figures signify profound insight and wisdom.

Palm sized identification mask

MINIATURE MASK

This wooden mask from northern Guinea is decorated with cowrie shells. It served as an identification mask for the local secret society of men, allowing members to identify themselves inconspicuously to other members.

In Africa, there were more secret societies of men than of women. Mixed groups, which admitted married couples, were even more rare. The members of such societies subjected themselves to a whole series of voluntary initiations. These initiations were distributed over the entire lifetime and coincided with the beginning of a new period of life. Membership brought many social and economic privileges. Thus, the societies of men claimed power over women and young people. Moreover, they assumed the right to hold court and to enforce judgments. Gatherings and rituals were kept strictly secret by all members. The secret societies were considered mediators between the living and the dead. Masks played an important role in their rituals. Only a few women were admitted to their festivities. Their task was to prepare the ritual millet beer that was consumed by the masked dancers. These women were called "sisters of the masks."

Because of their practice of oracle consultation and of healing rituals, the secret societies were considered preservers of tradition. The societies were generally respected and feared. Besides the power of the chieftains, they represented another influential power in the state. Thus, some countries in Africa owed their liberation from colonial domination to the activities of their secret societies. Even today, some politicians rely on their great influence.

Ritual mask, Nigeria

THE WATER SPIRIT OF THE IJO

The Ijo people live in the mangrove swamps on the western shore of the Niger delta. In order to gain the favor of the river god, dance ceremonies were held in his honor. Dancers wore these masks as they performed. The tribe of fishermen hoped that the ritual would secure a great catch. The mask represents the river spirit of the Niger. The faces of the god's children are carved into the lower end of the mask. They are responsible for the subsidiary branches of the river.

Mask of the secret society of women of the Mende tribe, Sierra Leone

SOWEI MASK

In its deeper significance, this mask of the Sande secret society of women from Sierra Leone represents the long deceased founder of the society. Only women who are both good dancers and higher members of the association wear this mask. A heavy cotton dress with thick black bunches of plants tied to it is worn along with it. The dance lasts two hours.

The carver would get the instruction from the leaders of the Sande alliance to create such a mask along with the order to keep it secret. After it was completed, the mask was smoothened with rough fig leaves and blackened with a special herbal extract, which was supposed to create the impression of healthy and shiny skin. The small face and the high forehead correspond to the female ideal of beauty among the Mende. In addition, there are the elaborate hairdo and the fleshy bulges on the neck, which represent beauty and fertility.

Although there existed a great number of secret societies of women in Africa, male societies were much more frequent.

Such alliances arose during the time of the dissolution of the primordial communities and of the matriarchy, when Christianity and Islam destroyed the old structures. Above all, they served to secure privileges for the members and often ruled in competition with the power of the chieftains. The ritual activities consisted mainly in the performance of mask dances, the singing of religious songs, and the communal presentation of offerings. Female secret societies existed in Mali, Upper Volta, Liberia, Sierra Leone, on the Ivory Coast, in the primeval forests and savannas of West, East, and Central Africa. The women usually put more emphasis on sculptures (frequently mother and child representations) than on the worship of masks.

The members of these female secret societies were very effective in standing their ground against the predominance of men. This predominance had its origin in the introduction of Christianity and of Islam. A man who married such a woman had to acknowledge her dominance. If he did not comply, his wife would besmirch herself with dirt or mud, wrap her body with reeds, run about on all fours, or beat everyone she met with a stick. Only by means of an offering or a present to the fetish of the society to which his wife belonged, was the husband able to put an end to her crazy antics and appease her. The woman would keep the largest part of the present for herself and end the whole affair with a joyous dance.

Mask for the initiation rites of the Dan-Ngere, Ivory Coast

MOTHER MASK

This Dan mask is used by the religious secret society of the Dan Ngere tribes living on the Ivory Coast. As the mother mask, it represents the ideal image of a beautiful woman. It has several tasks in the village and in the initiation camp. It is used to drive away witches and teach the myths, amongst other customs. The vertical line running from the base of the nose upwards through the center of the forehead, represents a scar tattoo that was common in earlier times among the men and women of these tribes.

The delicate facial features are a typical feature of the Dan masks. Every mask has its own name and is assigned certain tasks. During the initiation, for example, miniature masks were laid out on the path towards the gathering place. They were regarded as the representatives of the benevolent mask spirits of the region. A circumcisor could clean his knife from evil powers by touching such a miniature mask with the blade. The boys often tried their hand at carving small palm-sized masks, a process which was said to lead to dreams that divine the future. In this way, the spirits would tell the novice to become a mask dancer or a singer.

Among the Dan, women were not supposed to carry large masks with them. If a mask happened to be in their possession, they could order the carving of a miniature mask. Such a mask was then taken along when a woman, after her marriage, moved into the household of her husband. The miniature mask was kept hidden and thus ensured the connection to the powers of her ancestors.

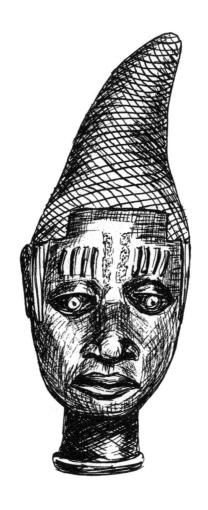

Representations of the female rulers of equal power

◆◆

THE QUEEN MOTHER

In most African tribes, the queen mother was an equal to the king. In important matters, she often had the power of decision making, and she was responsible for the election of a new king. In certain circumstances, she herself could take over the office of the king after his death.

In a metaphorical sense, the queen mother was considered the mother of all kings. The term designates much more an office than a family status. Only in rare cases was the queen mother really the mother of the king. She could be his sister, his aunt,or any other female member of the royal family who was considered capable of occupying this post. Often princesses, who, because of their noble descent were forbidden from marrying, were chosen to be queen mother. They were allowed to have children out of wedlock who could later likewise take over high or even the highest offices in the state.

The queen mother, as a rule, wielded great power, possessed much land, and her own royal retinue. She was also free to choose as many lovers or husbands as she liked. Officially, these were often called wives, as in the Lunda empire of the Congo area, for example.

(1) Brass head of a queen mother from ancient Benin. Only she was allowed to wear such a headdress. The offering signs on her forehead are very pronounced.

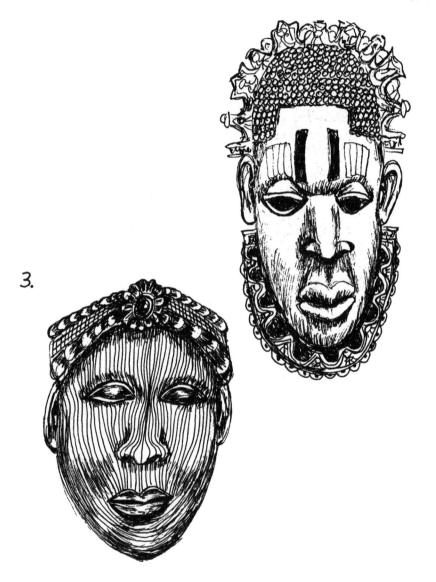

Representations of the Queen Mother

(2) This ivory mask of a queen mother likewise comes from Benin, although probably from a later era. On the ruff and on the headdress, one can see stylized heads of Portuguese. The Oba (king) carried this work of art on his belt. He thereby demonstrated his claim to the exclusive right of conducting trade relations with the foreigners. Again, the offering signs on the forehead are a typical feature.

(3) This representation comes from the empire of Ife, what is now southwestern Nigeria. It is a realistic portrait of the one-time ruler. The grooves in the brass sculpture covering the entire face represent either scar tattoos, a sign of beauty and rank, or a facial veil made of strings of pearls.

Mask for obsequies (Cameroon)

◆◆

RITUAL MASK

The elephant mask pictured here comes from the grasslands of Cameroon. It was worn during the obsequies of dancers. Traditionally, elephants embody wisdom and the office of chieftain. This mask is quite a large specimen with a length of approximately 70 cm. The mask is richly decorated with white and blue pearls. The basic colors are red and black, the traditional African colors of mourning. The white color of the pearls establishes the connection to the spirits. The accompanying three-quarter-length gown is opulently decorated with pearls and the hat, which completes the costume, is set with colorful feathers and has a diameter of approximately one meter.

Wearing such masks is supposed to establish a spiritual connection to the deceased. These masks did not necessarily have to be worn in front of the face, however. They could also be held by hand or attached to the back. Moreover, in this case, it was not important to keep the identity of the bearer of the mask secret. It was more a matter of raising the suspense of the situation and of maintaining a certain distance from the others. In smaller village communities everyone knew everyone else. This masks one's identity. In addition, there is the protective function which such a mask has for its bearer. It is supposed to protect the dancer from the evil eyes of the witches or the malevolent spirits and ancestors.

Large bird mask (Toma, Liberia)

◆◆

MYTHICAL BIRD

This large dance mask comes from the Toma, a Mende people, who live in Liberia and Guinea. The masks of the Mende peoples usually cover the entire head of the bearer. The example illustrated was carved from wood and decorated with bird feathers and plant fibers. The mixture of human and animal facial features is typical of this type of mask. As in ancient Greece, in Africa too, mixed beings were revered in many places.

Generally, a mask belongs to the spirit or god that it is supposed to represent. That is why the mask is accorded the same respect as the worshipped being itself. By means of the mask, the spirit communicates with the people. Thus, the bearer of the mask takes on the identity of the spirit and animates it with song and dance. His human personality recedes completely into the background so that he becomes the representative of the being. In a certain sense, the bearer becomes a half-god and enjoys a high regard in daily life as well. Masks were also used on other important occasions such as the administration of justice and legislation. In such a case, it is said that the mask has pronounced such and such, which means that the god himself has spoken, whereby the bearer of the mask served merely as a medium. Masks are either passed on from generation to generation or are newly produced every year. Very old masks are held in high regard, since they are also seen as connecting links to the ancestors.

Nkoh mask dress of the Kwifon secret society

KWIFON MASK

The Fons (kings) of the grasslands of Cameroon were not omnipotent rulers. Their decisions required the consent of the various secret societies, the most powerful of which was the Kwifon society. Kwifon means "carrying the king." Some ranks of the society are open to any person interested. The truly influential offices, however, are reserved for an elite based on birth, on wealth, or on special accomplishments. The Kwifon society constitutes a direct counterweight to the power of the king and is also responsible for determining his successor. It has many ritual objects and masks in its possession. In addition, the society possesses a magical instrument with which healings are performed and the souls of the deceased who cannot find peace are sent to the beyond.

The various masks of the Kwifon fulfill a variety of tasks in public appearances. Ahead of the procession, there is the runner mask, which announces the appearance of the Kwifon to the people and warns the uninitiated when dangerous rituals are about to take place.

The mask Nkoh, shown here, is the most dangerous and the most powerful of all the Kwifon masks. Prior to a performance, the bearer of this mask must take in a substance to rob him of his consciousness. Nkoh's appearance is always supervised by several experts in the art of healing. These magicians constantly spray him with a magical fluid.The mask always displays a distorted human face and represents wildness and aggressiveness. In public, Nkoh is usually held back by two men with ropes in order to protect the people and the bearer of the mask himself.

Runner mask of the Kwifon secret society

◆◆

MABUH THE RUNNER MASK

The masks of the various sub-groups of the Kwifon society fulfil a variety of tasks. Before the society makes a public appearance or performs dangerous and secret ceremonies, the runner mask goes out to warn the uninitiated population. All masks that appear in this way on behalf of the society are called Mabuh. The carved wooden mask sits on the head of the bearer, while his face is covered with a close-meshed net. He announces his appearance with a whistle. His gown reaches all the way to the ground and is covered with feathers everywhere, since birds are seen as spiritual messengers.

Mask embodying the nurturing female principle
(Dan, Ivory Coast)

DEA MASK

The Dea masks of the Dan are also called Deangle, meansing "eerie creature." Its task is to supply the young men who live in the initiation camps outside of the villages with food. The mask does not dance or sing, but it speaks to the villagers in a charming and graceful way. Usually, it begins to speak very softly and subsequently raises its voice more and more. This makes things difficult for people who do not want to fulfil their obligations towards the young men to be initiated. This Dea mask belongs to those lovely female masks, that reflect the ideal of beauty of the Dan.

Here we have a Dea mask with accompanying costume asking some women to bring food to the men who are about to be initiated.

Every mask of the Kwifon society has its own name and its own set of character traits.

Mask to ward off evil spirits (Ibibio, Nigeria)

BOGEYMASK OF THE IBIBIO

The Ibibio, neighbors of the Ibo, live in the forest around Nigeria's Cross River. This tribe has a bewildering wealth of artifacts. An expressive, often overdrawn, realism is a typical feature of the masks. Usually, their role is to banish the detrimental powers of evil spirits. There are masks of disease that often show distorted faces representing paralyses, or faces that are damaged by leprosy and gangrene. Skull-like designs, the effect of which is reinforced by a hinged jaw, can also be found frequently. Every village of the Ibibio is ruled by the Ekpo secret society. The mask shown here is one used by the society to instill fear and terror in the uninitiated.

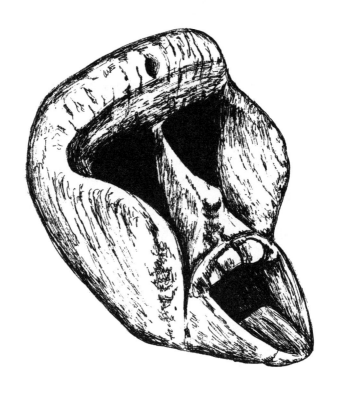

Bogeymask of the Guere, Ivory Coast

BUSH SPIRIT MASK

The Guere (or Ngere) prefer terrifying masks in order to drive away the dangerous bush spirits. Since these evil creatures are considered ugly, one tried to surpass them in this regard in representing them. The viciousness of the masks is always especially emphasized.

The Kaogle mask shown here has the task of testing loyalty towards the ruler. For no obvious reason, it attacks members of the tribe or destroys their property. The person who truly reveres and respects the tribal leader will not be truly angry about such an injustice. In addition, the mask was also used in the fight against bush spirits.

Mask representing the unity of all things

BAGA MASK

These masks represent supernatural beings from the world-view of the Baga people in Guinea. They make their appearance in initiation rituals. They are carried horizontally on the head, while the body of the dancer is completely covered by a long skirt of fibers.

The wood-carved masks of the Baga and the neighboring Nalu connect various areas of the history of creation and the worlds of experience; moreover, they are the embodiment of the unity of the universe. The mask combines the jaw of a crocodile, the horns of an antelope, and representations of a human face and of birds to create the impression during the dance that the mask can crawl, swim, and fly.

Imborirungu of the Tiv, Nigeria

ANCESTRAL RELIC

Most African communities assume that deceased persons who occupied important positions in life can get in touch with the living even after their death. It is often reported that the spirit of the ancestor can visit his descendants in the form of an animal (see also: animals). Traditionally, it is the duty of the head of the clan to cultivate the contact with the ancestors and to bring them offerings. In order to reach the ancestral spirits, who dwell in the "hidden world," he uses an Imborirungu (an instrument like the one displayed here). It is made from the skull and a thighbone of the deceased. The bone is fitted with the membrane of the wing of a bat and inserted into the mouth opening of the skull. The red and black seeds with which the ritual object is decorated represent stars, while cowrie shells form the eyes. Such an Imborirungu is treated with utmost respect and is generally kept hidden from outsiders. It is accessible only to the elders of the tribe. The construction makes it possible to generate sounds with the instrument that resemble the call of the screech owl. Owls are associated with superhuman powers.

The Imborirungu shown here from the Tiv in Nigeria is only used at night.

1.

2.

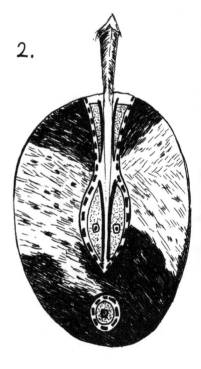

Symbols of wealth and luxury (Benin, Nigeria)

ROYAL FANS

Ornate leather fans were produced exclusively for the Oba (king) of Benin. They were important requisites in religious ceremonies. When the Oba presented himself in public, he had two servants constantly fanning him.

(1) This fan bears the emblem of sovereignty. Objects decorated with elephants belonged without exception to the king. The tusks were a symbol of luxury. If an elephant was killed, one of his tusks automatically became the property of the king.

(2) The second fan carries an application of red flannel ,which represents a mudfish. Fishermen caught huge numbers of these fish in the rivers, which made the mudfish a symbol of the abundance of the earth. A legend of the Edo (a people in Benin) even traced the origin of the people back to the mudfish. Objects representing these animals were reserved for the king.

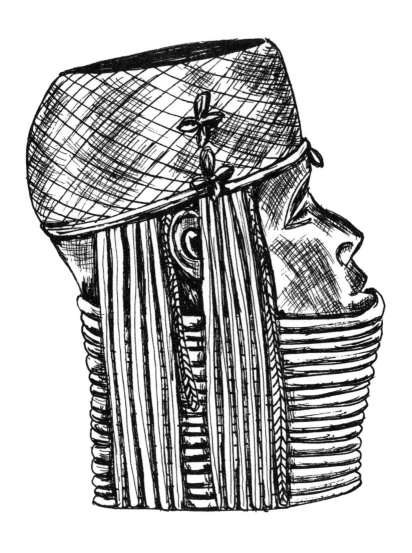

Elephant tusk holder as symbol of royal power (Benin)

HEAD OF A ROYAL ANCESTOR

This bronze sculpture is wearing the royal neck ornament of an Oba of Benin that covers almost half of the face. Only the king could order the production of such bronze heads in order to decorate his ancestral altar. This heavy head is designed in such a way that it could hold a 1.80 m long elephant's tusk, the symbol of a long life. It does not constitute a realistic portrait of a ruler, but rather the embodiment of the divine power that belonged to all Obas. The neck rings of the king, which he wore only once or twice a year during public appearances, consisted of coral pearls. The latter played an important role in the preservation of the royal power. In order to renew the magic power of the corals, the Oba would sprinkle them each year with the blood of a human sacrifice. The king was the only person in Benin who had the power over the life and death of a person.

Ceremonial vessel of the Bamum, Cameroon

ROYAL DRINKING VESSEL

On certain occasions, the Fon (king) of the Bamum empire would drink raffia palm wine from this decorated cattle horn. The double-headed brass snakes on the tip point to the fact that this is a ceremonial vessel. In the Bamum empire, brass was a metal to which only the king had a claim. He only allowed a few especially favored followers to wear or carry it.

When the Fon drank from the horn pictured here, he would always pour a few drops onto the ground as an offering to the ancestors resting below. The double-headed snakes are a symbol of royal power.

Royal throne of the Bamum, Cameroon

◆◆

THRONE OF THE KING'S MOTHER

Among the Bamum, the mother of the king was usually also his first advisor in matters of state. She used to sit to the left of her son on a throne such as this.

This stool carved from wood is completely decorated with pearls and cowrie shells. The blue, black, red, and white pearls were reserved for the royal family. The countless cowrie shells on the seat and on the foot of the throne symbolize wealth. They used to constitute the currency. A respectful human figure is bowing under the seat.

Symbol of power of the Ashanti, Ghana

◆◆

ROYAL STOOL

This is the chair of an Ashantehene (king) from the 19th century. It was carved from a single wooden block and decorated with silver bands. The curved seat is in the shape of the half moon and symbolizes the female energy. The seat rests on a circlar rainbow to reflect the all-encompassing dominion of the Ashantehene. The Ashanti have a saying, "The rainbow surrounds the neck of every people." The decorations at the outer edge of the rainbow represent the division of responsibilities. The zigzag patterns draw attention to the wisdom of the ruler.

In the entire Ashanti Empire, chairs of this kind are a symbol of political authority. The chairs of the chieftains are less magnificently decorated. It is said that the chair houses the energy of its owner, as well as the spirit of the tree from which it was carved. Only three types of tree could be considered for carving. Their spirit had to be pacified through the offering of an egg before they could be felled. After the completion of the work, the spirit was asked to move into the carved stool and regard it as its new home. After the death of its owner, such throne chairs were usually placed next to a tree of the kind from which its wood originated. Only the chairs of the king of the Ashanti were kept in the sacred rooms of the palace.

The greatest relic of the Ashanti is the legendary "golden stool," which the high priest Okomfo Anokye, is said to have brought from heaven in order to unite the Ashanti people. Since then, it is considered the seat of the soul of the Ashanti people. It is never used for sitting, but is rather kept in a secret place and is shown to the people only once every five years in a solemn procession.

Wooden throne of the Bamum, Cameroon

NJOYAS THRONE

The Fon (king) of the Bamum kingdom owned several throne chairs which resembled each other in symbolism and form. All of them were imitations of the European type of chair and were completely decorated with pearls and cowrie shells. Since the cowrie shells, which came from the Indian Ocean, used to be general currency in Africa, the Fon sat on a huge treasure. Many believe that the black, red, and white pearls probably had been brought by traders, because they are from Bohemia. Among the Bambara in Cameroon, pearl jewelry and objects decorated with pearls were reserved for the Fon.

The most important emblem of the king was the double-headed snake. It represented his ability to start fighting simultaneously in two directions with his army. The snake symbols on the back and on the base of the chair are richly decorated with pearls and cowrie shells.

Modern chair of government

MODERN SYMBOLISM IN CONTEMPORARY GHANA (1)

This is a chair of government whose star and two eagles stand for the state of Ghana. The geometrical pentagonal motif at the center of the star symbolizes the continued existence of the country. In the middle of the back, there is the Kerapa, a symbol of luck that is surrounded by three circles, the mark of the dignity of sovereignty. The red color of the seat cushion suggests life and strength. The right-angled arm rests express manliness and the zigzag lines signal wisdom and caution. The Adom symbol of divine grace is visible on the side panels, and the sign of the hearth of the house is carved into the base. The white wood of the chair, the embodiment of purity and innocence, has been completely covered with gold, the symbol of the dignity of sovereignty.

Throne of the sovereign of contemporary Ghana

MODERN SYMBOLISM IN CONTEMPORARY GHANA (2)

This figure shows the throne of government whose form is borrowed from the traditional Ghanaese chair. The seat in the shape of a lunar crescent represents the benevolent nature of the elephant, while the egg-shaped back represents perfection. Traditionally, the rainbow supporting the throne stands for the division of responsibilities. Underneath the rainbow, the slanted supports point to all the crooked things in the community. Like the stylized pineapple below, the black star of Ghana on the back proclaims the dominance of the nation as a whole over its individual regions. Inside the star, there is a circle describing the presence of God in society. Here too, the zigzag bands suggest wisdom and caution.

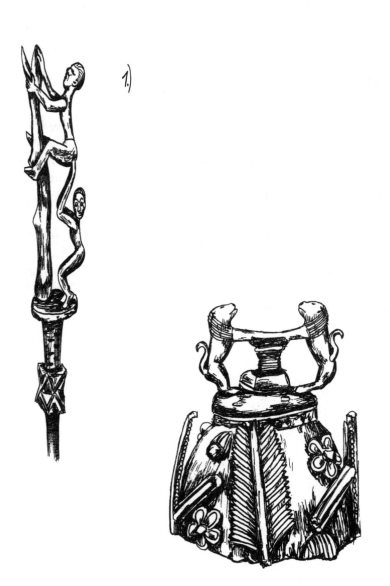

Symbols of honesty and courage (Ghana)

INSIGNIA OF THE ROYAL COURT OF THE ASHANTI

(1) The personal advisors of the Ashantehene (king) all carry long wooden staffs decorated with gold leaf as signs of their dignity. They are historical scholars, military experts, and speakers. The ornate staff tops usually provide a clue as to the task of their owners. Most often, the symbolism refers to a saying or a fable of the Ashanti. The staff depicted here recalls the popular saying "The person who takes the right and positive path will always receive help."

(2) This is the crown of an Ashantehene. It is completely covered with gold and decorated with the symbols of sovereign rule. The lions traditionally stand for boldness and strength. The fronds refer to stamina and fearlessness.

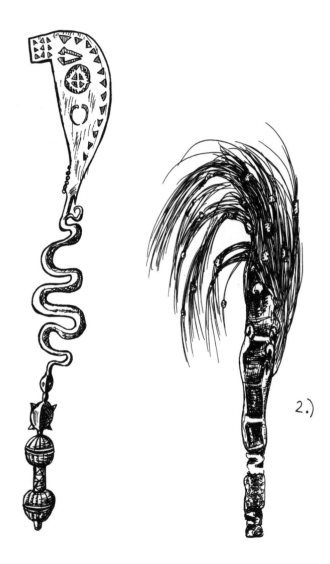

1.)

2.)

Symbols of authority (Ashanti, Ghana)

INSIGNIA OF THE ASHANTI RULERS

(1) Ceremonial swords are primarily used for display purposes. Above the gilded wooden handle, there is a turtle to show invincibility. It turns into a snake. This brings to mind the Ashanti aphorism: "The black Cobra is feared even when it has no evil intentions". The blade is decorated with geometrical ornaments. During public appearances, the Ashantehene (king) himself carried such a sword as an expression of his centralized power. The rulers of the Ashanti also swore a sacred oath on the sword when they took office.

(2) Fly whisks such as the one depicted here were used during official occasions. They are made from the tail of an elephant and attached to a golden handle. The symbolism goes back to the following Ashanti saying: "The tail of the elephant is short, but it drives away the flies." During royal processions, servants would use such whisks to drive away anything evil, while they were walking ahead of the ruler.

Ceremonial helmet of the Ashanti, Ghana

WAR HELMET OF THE ASHANTEHENE

In order to underscore also his position as commander-in-chief, he Ashantehene (king) wore this war helmet during his inaugura- ion. This ceremonial headdress is covered with the fur of an ante- ope and decorated with two tassels made from a lion's tail that ignal courage and strength. The golden jaw and head trophies tand for the conquered enemies. The royal power is expressed by he two horns. The palm branches at the crown of the helmet point o the fact that the strength of the king lies in the number of his sub- ects.

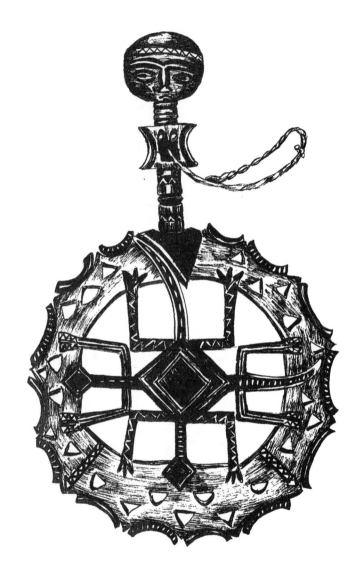

Ceremonial fan (Ghana)

WOODEN FAN OF THE ASHANTI

Blackened wood fans such as these were carried by the high ranking members of the Ashanti society during ceremonies of state. The circular form refers to God's omnipotence, while the curved or crescent-shaped decorations symbolize the female power. The zigzag ribbons indicate wisdom and caution. The crossed crocodiles are a common motif in Ashanti culture. They form the center of the fan and bring to mind the Ashanti proverb: "Crocodiles only have a stomach, but their heads fight over the food nonetheless." The angular shapes of the animals refer to the male energy. On the handle of the object, there is a symbol of fertility in the shape of an Akuaba doll.

Ritual Calabash of the Bamum, Cameroon

ROYAL CALABASH

This vessel comes from the Bamum Empire in Cameroon and belonged to the king. It consists of a bottle gourd (calabash) which is covered with fabric and embroidered with dark blue and white pearls. The cap is decorated by a striped chameleon; a symbol reserved for the nobility. The pattern on the belly of the bottle represents the earth spider, which has a special connection to the cult of the dead. Earth spiders were considered mediators between the living and the ancestors. Since they build their nests underground, one assumed that they could speak to the deceased. This is why soothsayers placed tiny pieces of wood around the hole of the spider. The spider moved the wood as it crawled out of its nest at night. From the arrangement of these pieces, the soothsayers would then read the message from the realm of the dead.

Only members of the upper class were allowed to use objects with the pattern of the spider, a pattern that represents wisdom. The calabash shown here was used to serve the wine of the raffia palm during state ceremonies or ritual acts.

Marks of social position (Cameroon)

◆◆

SYMBOLISM IN DRESS AND HAIRSTYLE

This Bamum woman from Cameroon is wearing her pewter wedding band on her forehead. Her hairstyle is an indication of her fertility; she has probably already born several children. The scar tattoos on her forehead give evidence of her membership in a certain tribe or clan. The more elaborate such tattoos (which can be found either on the body or on the face), the higher the social position of the person. In addition, there are certain tribe-specific signs that every member receives. Nowadays, such practices are in decline, and the meaning of the tattoos has largely been forgotten.

In traditional African society, all things and acts have magic significance. Thus, circumstances of life, inner dispositions, and states of mind are outwardly expressed through dress, ornaments, hairstyle, and body painting. In this regard, there are numerous tribe-specific peculiarities of which only some examples have been given here.

Soothsaying instrument from Nigeria

TOOLS OF THE IFA ORACLE

In Nigeria, the Yoruba name Ifa refers to the god of wisdom, knowledge, and soothsaying. According to an old myth, Ife came to earth with other gods just when the earth was being created. His wisdom contributed towards creating order. He settled in Ile Ife, a place in what is now West Nigeria, married, and fathered eight children. These children all became supreme chieftains and ruled the Yoruba land. Since heaven and earth were still very close at that time, Ifa often traveled home in order to advise the other gods. When one day he was insulted by one of his sons, he decided not to return to earth, whereupon the world was thrown into terrible chaos. The desperate people sent out his eight children in order to sway Ifa to return. But he refused. Instead, he gave each of his children 16 cola nuts with the help of which they would now be able to tell the future. Since then, Ifa proclaims the will of the gods to the people in this way, and, in turn, transmits the requests of the people to the gods.

Illustration (1) shows a wooden soothsaying staff that was tapped against the edge of the wooden board (illustration 2). The cola nuts distributed over a bed of sand on this oracle board moved due to the blow of the staff. The priest would then read from the resulting image. The oracle could give information about the future or advice on business matters as well as help settle disputes.

Instrument for the invocation of the ancestors (Ogboni, Nigeria)

BRASS RATTLE

This rattle was used by the Ogboni secret society in the Oyo Empire. It served to call the ancestral spirits during secret rituals. The representation of faces is typical for this secret society; it is the same in all ritual objects. The images of man (top) and woman (bottom) are shown here in their union, represented by the handle in the middle. The Ogboni society included men as well as women. It was the most influential alliance of the Yoruba speaking tribes in Nigeria. As such, it oversaw the selection of the new king, as well as the dismissal of kings and dignitaries. It rendered judgment and had the power of imposing the death sentence. In the Oyo empire, the king, the priests, and the Ogboni secret society ruled in equal measure. The king represented the heavens, the Ogboni the earth, and the priesthood the people. The Ogboni served the god of the earth and were thus independent of the other gods. Their spiritual powers were feared.

The rattle represents the founding couple of the society. The eyes of all the Ogboni figures are always greatly magnified, which is supposed to indicate inner vision and wisdom. The most important basic theme of this society was the cooperation of man and woman. On the foreheads of the faces of the object shown here, we see the symbol of duality, the all-encompassing unity which falls into opposites: two mirror images of lunar crescents.

The art of the Ogboni usually combined brass and iron. Brass stood for femininity, iron for masculinity.

The earth was the common abode of the ancestors of both sexes.

173

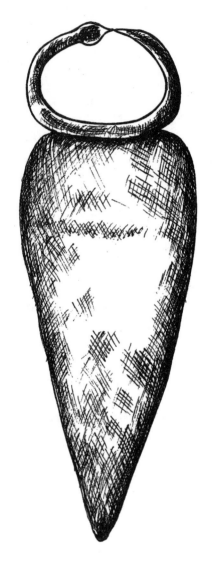

Ritual knife for the initiation rites (Ghana)

CIRCUMCISION KNIFE OF THE AKAN

This ritual knife made out of metal, like most utensils of the Akan-speaking people, bears a symbol, which points to a proverb. The bird turning its head backward means: "If you want to know where you are going, then see where you are coming from."

In Africa, circumcision was prevalent for several reasons. In most black African tribes, as with the Akan, circumcisions are only carried out on men for hygienic reasons. In the Islamized and Christianized areas, however, female circumcisions are also common. Islam prescribes circumcisions for men so that they may enter paradise. Since African women generally have a very equal status, the Muslim people wanted to make it possible for them to enter the heavenly kingdom. For this reason, the circumcision of young girls was introduced in many places on the occasion of the initiation ceremonies. The tribe of the Dogon in Mali believes that through the initiation, every human being should have an unambiguous gender. For this reason, the foreskin of the man (which resembles a vagina) and the clitoris (resembling a penis) were to be removed. In other tribes, by contrast, it was thought that the clitoris would impede conception and birth.

Instrument for initiation rituals (Ivory Coast)

THE RING OF SILENCE

This buffalo head cast in bronze was used by the Senufo people on the Ivory Coast. If at certain times a candidate was to remain silent during an initiation ritual, he would put such a ring in his mouth.

Symbol of royal authority (Ghana)

CHEST PLATE OF THE ASHANTI

This badge, made from very fine gold, was worn by the priests of the Ashanti who accompanied the Ashantehene, or king, and carried the golden chair. Often it is referred to as the sign of the soul washer, since it was also worn by the Okra of the chieftain, who had the task of cleaning the soul of the head of the tribe.

These plates had many applications, however. In various versions, they were worn by courtiers or by girls during the ceremonies of passage into adulthood. Today, they might mark one of the main mourners at a burial ceremony. They were originally worn on a white string around the neck.

The filigreed patterns of these badges were obtained by means of wax engravings that were subsequently cast in gold. As a whole, this chest plate is a symbol of the power of the chieftain: the circle is the earth, the four protrusions indicate the directions. The four arrows united in the middle represent a crossroad. They refer to the following proverb from the Akan language: "The chieftain is like a crossroad, all paths lead to him."

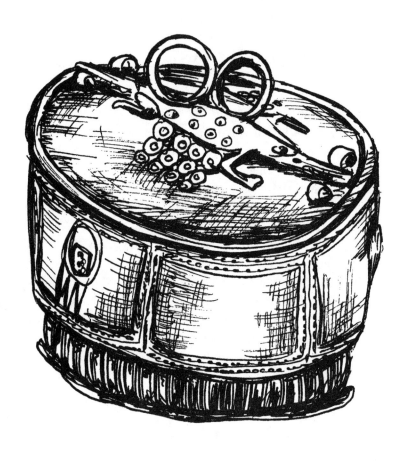

Ashanti vessel for the storage of gold dust, Ghana

KUDUO

Brass containers like this served for the storage of gold dust or personal valuables. After the death of their owner, they were frequently passed along into the grave. Some were also used as ritual vessels during important political and cultural events. In that case, they were usually kept in the hallowed halls of the palace where the throne chairs of the previous rulers were also found. The usually very ornate Kuduos were always coveted status symbols in the noble Ashanti society. The artists of the Akan tribes duplicated containers that Arabic tribes used as jewelry vessels. The Kuduo pictured here has been fitted with the bas-relief of a double-headed crocodile on the lid. Crocodiles are usually regarded as guardians of justice. The proverb that goes with this motif says: "At the end of each year, the old crocodile always swallows a stone." This means that every year a misfortune occurs which people must accept as part of life. One was especially concerned that the lid of the Kuduo was closed tightly, for any gold dust that spilled onto the ground legally belonged to the Ashantehene (king). The latter regularly had his servants sweep the streets and squares to gather the gold dust, something that the population was strictly forbidden to do.

Posture of respect carved into pillars (Bamum, Cameroon)

PILLARS AT THE HOUSE OF THE KING OF THE BAMUM

These pillars carved from wood supported the roof of the royal terrace. The figures are almost life-size and are displayed resting chin on hand, a traditional gesture of respect. The house behind them was inhabited only by the king. A subject could easily pay with his life if he did not demonstrate sufficient respect to the Fon (king). Thus, no mortal was allowed to see the king perform mundane activities such as eating and drinking. For a god-like ruler such as the Fon officially had no need for such things. In spite of his divinity, however, the king of the Bamum was quite a worldly ruler, holding audiences every day. Every subject, whether slave or nobleman, would find him ready to listen. The Fon Njoya, who lived at the beginning of our century, was the only ruler in black Africa to develop a writing system for his people, one which comprised eighty signs and ten numerals.

1.

2.

Moorish wall reliefs from Qualata ,Mauritania

WALL DECORATION

Illustration (1) shows a classical Moorish wall relief from the town of Qualata in the southwest of Mauritania. Unlike in other areas of Africa, among the Moors, the decorations are not made by the lady of the house, but by female servants or the wives of the trades people. Women of the noble upper class never take on such work. Even today, the city of Qualata is still a unique island of Moorish building tradition.

Wall reliefs are made from clay and painted with earth colors. The pattern depicted here is called "mother with thighs". In endless links, it repeats a certain part of the female thigh. Most patterns are derived from body parts, activities, or Arabic letters and transferred into symbolic representations. These wall decorations serve primarily aesthetic purposes.

The mural painting shown in illustration (2) combines the motif of the sun (bottom left) with the typical Islamic lunar and stellar ornaments. The only purpose of this type of painting is the beautification of the room to which it is applied. The walls of the houses of the Soninke in Mauritania are usually completely decorated with such patterns, which form a charming contrast to the otherwise barren surroundings. Islam prohibits the representations of figures. Hence, one finds only stylized representations and ornaments in the mural paintings of Mauritania.

Wall decorations

DECORATIONS ON THE WALLS OF HOUSES

(1) As a symbol of hospitality, a sheaf of millet has been suspended over the entrance of a residential house of the Kassena in Navrongo. The millet will later be prepared and offered to the guests.

The pattern running in parallel and diagonal lines at the upper and lower edge is called Gwenu, which means furrows. The zigzag lines in the center area are called Togo-Naga and represent deer legs. Traditionally, the women create the paintings. The colors are white, a symbol of purity, and black. They consist of chalk and coal tar, which also serves as a disinfectant. The low entrance has the effect that the interior of the house is cool, dry, and protected against outsiders. This effect is reinforced by a low wall that was constructed immediately behind the entrance in the interior of the house.

(2) Here we see a typical wall ornamentation from Upper Volta. It was created by pressing corn cobs into wet clay. The pattern stands for longevity and also serves to drain off rain.

Mural paintings from Ghana and Upper Volta

MURAL PAINTINGS FROM THE BORDER AREA
BETWEEN GHANA AND UPPER VOLTA

(1) The upper half of this wall of a building in Sirigu (Ghana) features the pattern of the broken calabash (bottle gourd). The lower part shows a stylized calabash net. Both motifs are important symbols of femininity.

(2) The royal drinking house of the Kassena in Upper Volta is richly decorated with symbols. On the left part of the picture, we see the motif of the handshake, which stands for unity and hospitality. The triangular patterns found on almost all walls of the region stand for the broken calabash, that is, for femininity. In addition, there is a stylized hourglass drum. The mural paintings generally speak of the role of the woman and her environment.

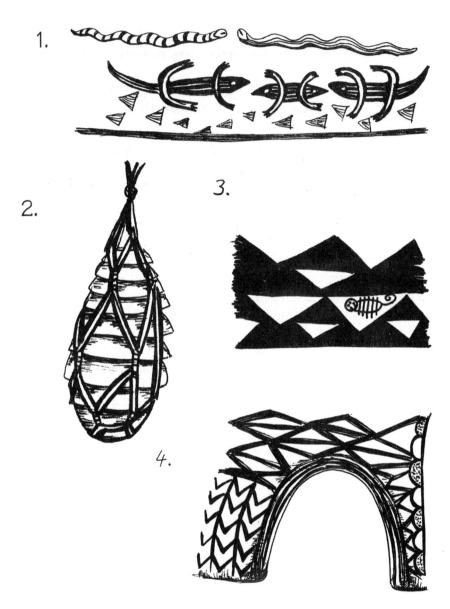

Symbolic ornamentation on houses in Ghana and Upper Volta

(1) Relief on the wall of a house in Tiébélé in Upper Volta. It features three crocodiles. The double-headed crocodile in the middle represents a god of the earth and the waters who is accompanied by a male and a female crocodile. Above them, there is a picture of a male and a female python symbolizing Adam and Eve. The triangular pattern of the broken calabash (femininity) forms the background.

(2) Calabash net, as it is used in the original African households.

(3) Inside this calabash net pattern there is a single scorpion which is supposed to remind the children not to play with it.

(4) The entrance area of this house in Sirigu (Ghana) is decorated with many different patterns. In the upper area, one can see the classical net for carrying calabashes. The V-shaped motif at the bottom on the left is a greeting sign for visitors. It derives from the familiar picture of the handshake. The crescent-shaped drawings on the right edge represent the hairstyle of an old woman.

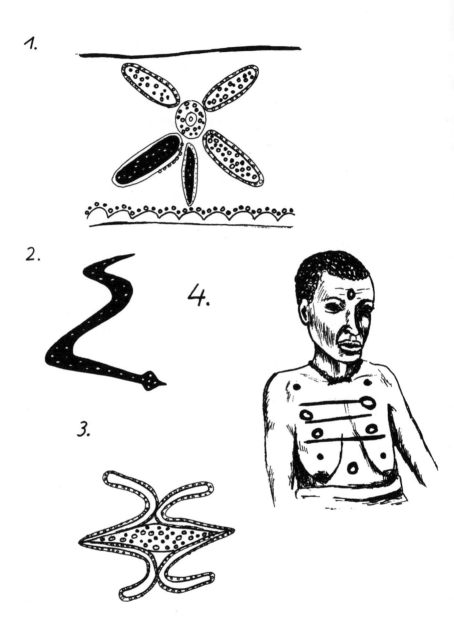

Female symbolism in mural paintings and body paintings of the Igbo, Nigeria

MURAL PAINTINGS IN NIGERIA

(1) Here we have a typical female motif: a rudder underneath a four-rayed sun. The rays stand for the four delegates of God who were sent to earth on the four market days. Women are traditionally responsible for business in the marketplace.

(2) Among the Igbo, the python embodies a daughter and for this reason is never hunted. Daughters have the responsibility of settling disputes between families. When a woman dies a python is sacrificed for the divinity.

(3) This motif shows a stylized Yams beetle the back of which has been decorated with Uli ornaments. Uli ornaments are signs painted on women's bodies or incorporated in animal representations on the walls of houses.

(4) A woman who wears the Uli pattern is regarded as good by the other women of the community. Uli motifs are found in body painting and on murals.

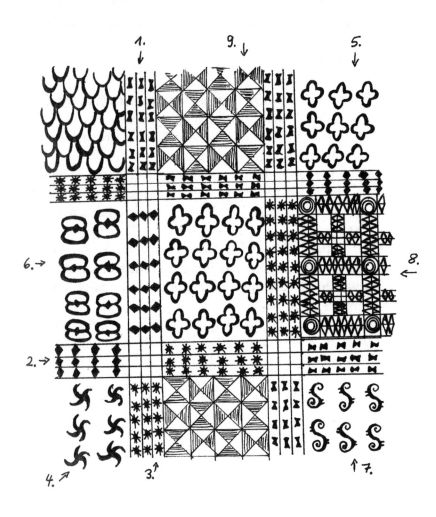

Fabric of a court costume of the Ashanti, Ghana

DETAIL OF A PRINTED FABRIC

Among the Ashanti, court costumes in black and white such as the one displayed here were worn only on solemn occasions like funerals. Fabrics of this kind were reserved for members of the royal court. The printing blocks were created from parts of a calabash (a type of pumpkin which, hollowed, is worked into a variety of useful and ritual objects). An extract from the bark of a tree served as printing color. These fabrics were printed with stylized plant and animal ornaments as well as with symbols which expressed a proverb. There were also cloths decorated with a single motif and worn by the Ashantehene (king) in order to make a political statement without speaking many words.

The triple rows partitioning the fabric show drums (1), diamonds (2), and stars (3). The field in the lower left corner (4) shows the symbol of the willingness to serve. Yam, a staple food of the Ashanti, is represented as a cross-shaped sign. It is found at the center and in the corner on the upper right (5). At the center on the left (6), we find a pattern that symbolizes a prayer: "God, allow me to partake in good and heavenly things." The sign on the lower right (7) shows the hairdress of a hero and symbolizes his courage. The pattern in the center part on the right is composed of various symbols (8). The threefold circles stand for magnanimity and steadfastness, the zigzag ribbons stand for wisdom. At the center at the top and at the bottom, we see patterns which refer to stability (9). (See also: Adinkra symbols)

Magical gown (Ivory Coast)

PAINTED CLOTH

This cloth is part of the costume of the fire-breather of the Senufo. During the dance, which takes place in darkness, red-hot coals and sparks would spring from the mask of the actor. This is why the Europeans referred to the Senufo as "fire-breathers." At the center of the fabric, there is a representation of the dancer wearing the mask of the fire-breather. He is surrounded by magical symbols, stylized lizards and turtles. The turtle is considered invincible, the lizard a sign of masculinity.

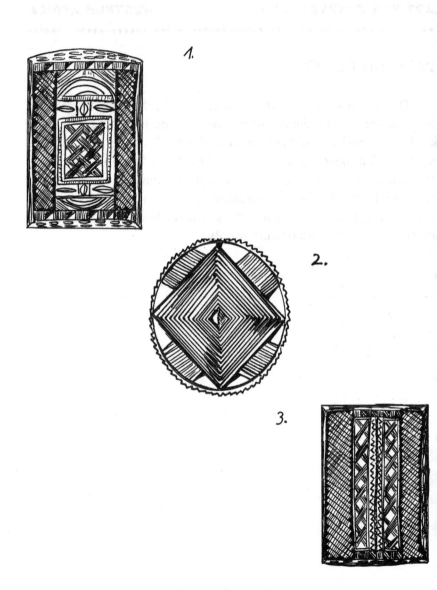

Book covers from Nigeria

PAPERWEIGHTS

Here are three examples of wooden paperweights from Nigeria. They come from Nupe and were used to cover valuable parchment papers such as the Koran. These so-called Panko book covers are nowadays remodeled into mirror frames.

Most of the carved ornaments are merely of a decorative nature, as in illustration (3). The ornamentation in illustration (1), on the other hand, points to influences of Islam, recognizable by the crescent-shaped lines. The pattern at the center also reveals that the object was made for a higher dignitary.

The pattern of the Panko book cover (2) is rather typical for the northern areas of Africa. It is a symbol of the four directions or the four corners of the world.

GOLDEN WEIGHTS

The golden weights of the Akan-speaking tribes were usually made of brass. Customers commissioned an artist to produce them. They then determined their weight. There exists an astounding variety of these little objects. The forms vary from simple geometrical representations to utensils of daily life to images of plants and animals. Many golden weights also derive from proverbs. Besides the brass weights shown here there were also sham weights consisting of plant seeds, shells, or small metal parts such as cartridge cases.

(1) A weight in the form of a stool such as every member of the Akan-speaking tribes owned in former times. A stool like this was a status symbol. Fathers passed these on to their sons and the young women would then receive them from their husbands at the wedding. If their owner died, they were blackened with sacrificial blood. If the deceased was a high dignitary, these stools became ancestral stools.

(2) Forked posts such as the one displayed here served as back support for the king as he sat on a cushion during funeral ceremonies. Similar posts were also used to hold the offering bowls in

buildings.

(3) The representation of the knot of wisdom exists in different variations. It is based on the proverb: "When you are weaving and the threads get entangled, you need both hands to disentangle them." This means that even a wise man can use the help of another when he has a problem to solve.

(4) This weight carries the following message: "How can you expect to see Nyame (God) lying with your face to the ground, when even I cannot see him, even though I am lying on my back."

(5) Here we see the representation of an offering scene: A priest offers eggs to a god or spirit. The egg is also the subject of several proverbs, for example: "The egg says: I am like authority. If you squeeze me too hard, I break. If you let me go, I fall to the ground and burst."

(6) The woodpeckers on the tree always want the tree to die so that they can chisel holes into it.

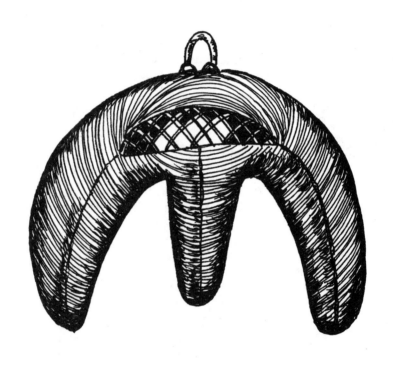

Symbol combining the powers of the moon with those of the ram
(Ashanti, Ghana)

MOON AMULET

Among the Ashanti, this golden pendant is worn on the head by chieftains and kings. It represents a combination of the lunar crescent and the horns of the ram. Among the Akan-speaking tribes, the ram symbolizes the god of thunder, while the lunar crescent stands for rain and water.

In ancient times, the lunar goddess was worshipped throughout Africa. In more recent times, however, this worship has all but disappeared. In East Africa, as in ancient Egypt, black cats are associated with the moon. Cats are symbols for spirited young girls. There is also a story that tells of a time when the moon was much closer to the earth and shone brighter. Through the poisoned arrow of a bushman, it was weakened and finally died. The Nuer in Sudan call the moon the daughter of the god of the heavens, and the kings of Burundiare descended from the lunar goddess. They are also convinced that they will return to the moon after their death. Many tribes pray for good health, fertility, and rain on the days of the new moon. Lunar eclipses are generally interpreted as a bad omen, because the angry moon does not want to show itself.

In summary, one can say that the moon embodies the female powers and is responsible for the water supply of the earth. The lunar goddess was probably the first deity worshipped on the African continent. She was an important component of the old matriarchically organized societies.

The moon brings human beings the promise of rebirth. For, like the moon, people are to disappear and return in an eternal cycle

◆◆◆

Adinkra symbols

The Adinkra symbols of the Ashanti in Ghana are timeless and still used today. There are contradictory views as to their origin and age. The name "Adinkra" can probably be traced back to the word "Dinkra" of the Akan language, which is also spoken by the Ashanti. "Dinkra" means: being separated, taking leave, saying farewell. Fabrics printed with the Adinkra motifs are often used during times of mourning. Approximately four hundred such symbols are known in Ghana, although the meaning of many of them has been lost. Normally, the Adinkra are simplified or stylized representations of objects, plants, animals, natural shapes, hairstyles, or buildings. Many of these motifs share a common basic form, and slight variations in the representation may entail a change in the meaning. Adinkra motifs were frequently employed as transmitters of certain messages and were used in art, as decorations on the walls of buildings, and in the printing of fabrics. Often they also reflect proverbs, which play a great role in the daily life of the Ashanti and which reveal much about their philosophy and their moral values.

The following chapter lists 62 of the best known Adinkra symbols still in use today.

1.

(1) This is one of the signs for "Nyame" which admonishes people not to fear anything except God. It is the highest of the Adinkra symbols and describes the all-encompassing God and his omnipotence.

2.

(2) Another popular symbol shows a bird turning around to catch its lost egg. It is a sign of the return, which says that it is never too late to turn around and start on a new path once one has recognized one's mistake.

A second meaning derives from the following Ashanti proverb: "Look at your past and you will recognize your future."

1.

(1) This is the sign for greatness in every relationship. The four dots indicate the four directions.

2.

(2) The symbol of the archer stands for bravery.

3.

(3) This precise grid pattern refers to accuracy and uprightness.

4.

(4) This symbol is supposed to convey purity and luck by invoking the presence of God.

5.

(5) The purity of the soul is represented in this form. This is the sign of spirituality.

(6) A person who teaches another person with patience is characterized with this symbol. It also stands for compassion and protection.

6.

1.

(1) Dauntlessness and courage are symbolized by this sign. It indicates the will to persist even when adverse circumstances make it difficult. Towards the top, the obtrusive influences get smaller. This means that when one continues on the chosen path without wavering, the difficulties will diminish as well.

2.

(2) Symbol of the eyes of the king. It stands for the omnipresence of the king in his realm of power. For his eyes see everything.

3.

(3) This sign could be "awarded" for outstanding achievements. In Ashanti culture, it represents a high honor.

4.

(4) This is a stylized representation of the king's rifle. It refers to the greatness and power of the king.

5.

(5) This is the sign of mutual responsibility in which, however, neither party has to surrender his or her individuality. It also represents cooperation.

6.

(6) The symbol of united hearts. It stands for solidarity.

1.

5.

3.

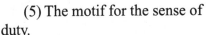

2.

4.

6.

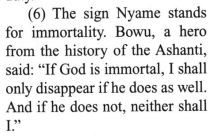

(1) This sign, which is used in a continuous pattern, is supposed to serve as a reminder that a serious facial expression is not necessarily a sign of irritation and anger.

(2) The representation of the latter of death is supposed to remind people that they all have to go the same way in the end.

(3) The stylized hairdress of a hero stands for bravery and fearlessness.

(4) The symbol of abundance is composed of four simplified cowrie shells. These rare shells were the accepted currency in ancient Africa.

(5) The motif for the sense of duty.

(6) The sign Nyame stands for immortality. Bowu, a hero from the history of the Ashanti, said: "If God is immortal, I shall only disappear if he does as well. And if he does not, neither shall I."

1.

(1) The moon and the stars stand for gentle characteristics such as loyalty, mercy, and trust.

2.

(2) This symbol embodies pride and greatness. Yet it also warns against haughtiness.

3.

(3) Two crossed crocodiles invoke unity in multiplicity. It is one of the most commonly used symbols in Ghana. It appeals for solidarity and tolerance. The sign also tells us that one mind alone cannot decide for many.

(4) The seal of the law. It stands for justice (in the sense of laws created by humans beings) and authority.

4.

5.

(5) This symbol pointing in all four directions refers to strength, endurance, and confidence.

(6) The readiness to learn and to develop wisdom are signaled with this sign. Thus, it also shows humility.

6.

1.

(1) Magnanimity, stead-fastness, and conscientious-ness are described in this form.

2.

(2) The crossed ceremonial swords of the king refer to the authority of government.

3.

(3) The strongly simplified motif of a solidly built and well-ventilated house.

(4) This sign contains a warning against envy. It shows a stylized Foofoo seed. Foofoo is a kind of grain and an im-portant nutritional component.

4.

(5) A bundle of cola nuts symbolizes wealth and abun-dance.

5.

(6) Uprightness is signi-fied by five evenly distributed circles.

6.

1.

2.

3.

4.

5.

6.

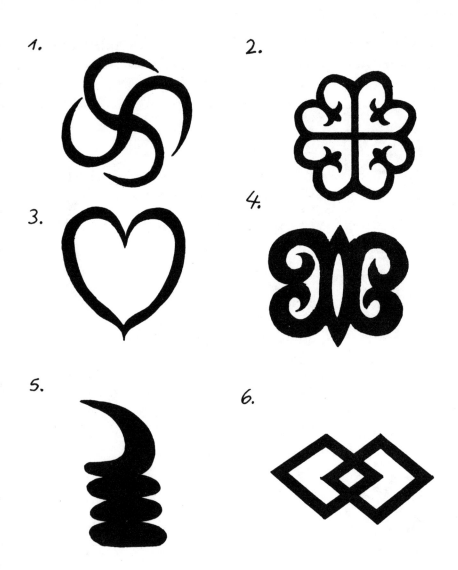

Symbolic language of the Ashanti, Ghana

◆◆

(1) The stylized hairdress of the female servants of the queen mother stands for readiness to serve.

(2) This symbol reminds people of God's omnipresence.

(3) Benevolence, firmness of character, and patience are associated with this sign.

(4) Pempamsee, the sign of indestructibility and strength of the community, is associated with the following saying: "A broom bound with ties of blood, loyalty, and mutual care. A dress of many colors, sown as a sign, as strength. Whoever isolates himself may see his dwarfish strength break, his beauty split up and incomplete."

(5) This stylized war horn signalizes readiness for battle.

(6) The simplified handcuffs recall the fact that the law stands above the people

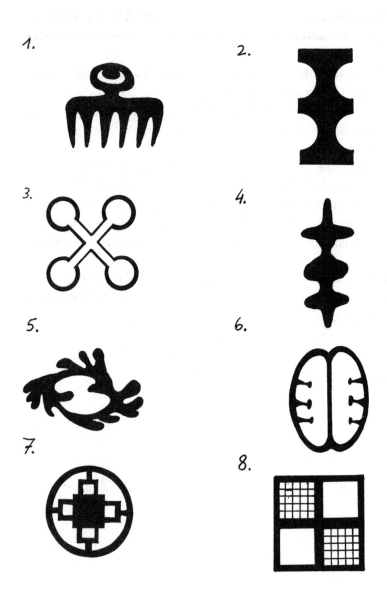

1.

2.

3.

4.

5.

6.

7.

8.

Symbolic language of the Ashanti, Ghana

(1) The stylized comb refers to the feminine virtues of consideration, caution, circumspection, and tenderness.

(2) This sign embodies the characteristics of vigilance, agility, and cheerfulness.

(3) This symbolizes the immortality of the soul represented as a closed unity.

(4) This symbol stands for physical and mental-spiritual strength.

(5) The virtues of justice and honesty are united in this motif.

(6) This sign points out that our life is characterized by community with others and our dependence on others. It also reminds us of how important kindness is in our dealings with each other.

(7) Intelligence and roguishness are represented in this way.

(8) A historical sign which stands for a group

Symbolic language of the Ashanti, Ghana

(1) The symbol of the star reminds us that we are all God's children.

(2) This sign describes a person who is selflessly ready to fulfil his or her duties. It also expresses as certain kind of unyieldingness.

(3) This pattern speaks of wisdom and the knowledge of the connections of things and of the order of the world. In addition, it refers to careful behavior.

(4) This symbol speaks of the ability to perform heroic deeds. It also contains the admonition to be careful and discreet about it.

(5) This refers to the firmness and the power of self-assertion of a self-confident person.

(6) This is the stylized representation of a house that suggests security and protection.

(7) This simplified image of a drum might represent either a war drum or a drum that tells the time. In the past, the time of day was determined among the Ashanti by the length of a person's shadow and in some places announced by means of drumbeats.

(8) This sign describes the power that extends over the four directions as well as over the four elements. In addition, it stands for respect for the law in these areas.

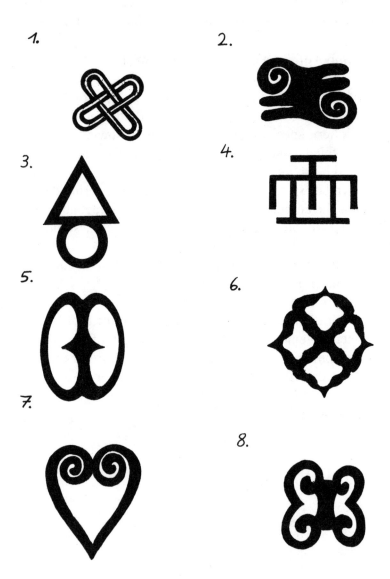

1.

2.

3.

4.

5.

6.

7.

8.

Symbolic language of the Ashanti, Ghana

(1) This symbolic entanglement is to be understood as a warning against hypocrisy and falseness.

(2) The back of the head of Chieftain Gyawus is represented in this stylized form. The motif reminds people of his flight.

(3) Here we see the knife of the executioner in simplified form.

(4) All goods produced in Ghana carry this sign as a quality seal. It stands for perfection and the associated abhorrence of imperfection.

(5) The union with God and the associated trust in divine guidance.

(6) An enclosure in stylized form. It is supposed to evoke associations of security and love.

(7) This symbol reminds people that the future is built upon the past.

(8) Here we see the sign of steadfastness and readiness.

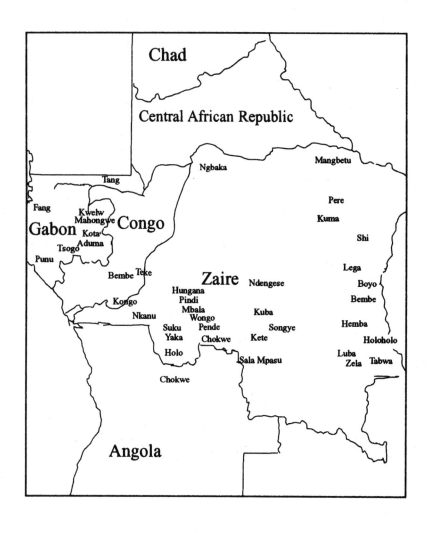

THE CENTER

CHAD

CENTRAL AFRICAN REPUBLIC

CONGO

GABON

ZAIRE

ANGOLA

Mask that announces the end of the initiations (Basuku)

INITIATION MASK

This mask of the Basuku, a tribe of the Bayaka people, is designed as a helmet mask. It is crowned by an animal that probably represents a small bush antelope. The white face mask stands for the realm of the spirits from which the young people to be initiated are reborn. The uses of such masks were quite diverse. They were worn by the young men to be initiated themselves, who made each other laugh through clownery and contortions. Or, the leaders of the initiation ritual wore them in order to announce to the village the end of the isolation and initiate the subsequent festivities. The mask shown here was put into action during the initiation of young men. Similar masks were made for the initiation of the girls.

Initiation masks that embody an ideal picture of the human being (Batshokwe, Congo)

MAKISHI MASKS

(1) Among the Lunda-Batshokwe in southern Congo, such masks were worn by the sons of the chieftain. They performed during the Makishi initiation dances in order to illustrate the power and the wealth of the chieftain. The mask, representing the chieftain himself, was also worn during the fertility rites and during the investiture of the king. It was made from wood and raffia palm fibers. The disk at the chin indicates a beard.

(2) Here we see the female counterpart. Both masks were put on during the Pwo fertility dances. It is the representation of a young woman who has just returned from the initiation school in the forest. She then expresses her readiness for marriage. The powerful corporeal forms exuding peace and dignity are typical of the representations of the Batshokwe. This inner peace shows the human being in harmony with himself or herself and the cosmos

Moshamboy mask representing the divinity of the king (Kuba, Zaïre

MASK OF THE KING

Among the Kuba, Moshamboy masks represented the king who also owned them. The Nyim (king) acted as an advisor in the production of this mask. In the opinion of the people, the mask had the same magical powers as the king himself. During festivities, it was worn by the Nyim or by an authorized high dignitary. Copper plates, pearls, and cowrie shells are signs of wealth, and they cover almost the entire mask. The personal wealth of the Nyim was the pride of the whole people who had elevated him to a god-like being.

During ritual dances, the king took on the role of the Woot. The Woot myth describes the victory over the Pygmies and the building of a new empire in the newly acquired land. The Moshamboy mask illustrates the divine origin of the Nyim. (See also following page.)

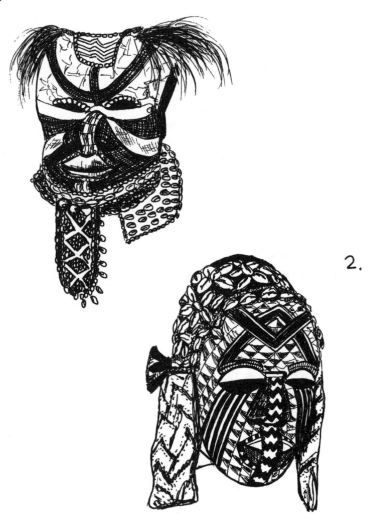

Mythical dance masks (Zaire)

MALE AND FEMALE MASK OF THE KUBA

Both of these masks were worn on the occasion of the presentation of the Woot myth. The Kuba, in Zaire, called such masks the fantastic friends of the king". While the king wore the Moshamboy mask during the dance, a dancer with a Bwoom mask embodied the ordinary man, and a third, wearing a Ngaadi-a-mwaash mask, represented the female side.

(1) This Bwoom mask was made from heavy leather and decorated with copper and pearls. It completely enclosed the head of the dancer. Since there are no openings for the eyes, the performer had to dance blindly. The respect-instilling facial expression is a typical feature of the Bwoom masks. This is how the ordinary man was presented in the dance. During the performance of the Woot myth, this mask represented the Pygmies who were once conquered by the Woot. Their characteristic facial features are likewise reflected in the mask.

(2) In the Woot myth, this Ngaadi-a-mwaash mask represents the sister of the Woot. She generally symbolizes the female sex. The tear traces on the cheeks of the mask show the fear women have of war and the sufferings of childbirth. A strip of pearls seals the lips.

Spirit mask

TEBO MASK

For the Bakongo and neighboring tribes in Zaire, the word Tebo" refers to an evil spirit. The spirit has the appearance of an ugly and wrinkly dwarf, and he makes himself visible from time to time in order to frighten the people in the villages and farmsteads. Tebos steal livestock, and they attack people who are travelling alone in the forest in order to eat them in their caves. They can also appear incognito in the shape of an animal. In such a case, only a sorcerer who owns a powerful fetish can recognize them. If he likes, he can then enslave a Tebo and bring him to carry out murders on his instructions. It is also reported that black magicians who have caused the death of a person for selfish reasons were transformed into Tebos; after their death, the ancestors barred them from entering the realm of the dead.

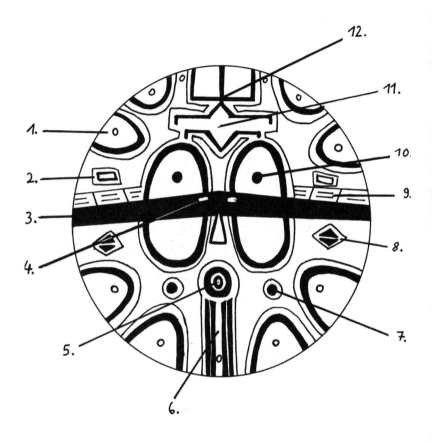

Dance mask of the BaTeke, Congo

◆◆

IASK ORNAMENTS: TSAYE MASK OF THE BA EKE

A symbolism full of meaning often hides behind the rich orna-
ients of African masks. The meanings, however, have frequently
zen lost, or the signs have been altered so much that they are
ardly readable today. This sign language is different for each tribe.
or example, this is the decoding of a Tsaye dance mask. of the Ba
eke tribe who live in the Congo near the border of Gabon. All
ymbols are strongly simplified and encoded.

(1) This sign represents one half of the moon. The four of them
t half mask stand for one week, which consists of four days.

(2) The mirror, symbol of defense

(3) The eyebrows or eyelashes are represented as a wide hori-
ontal beam. In the middle, we find the triangular nose.

(4) The eyes

(5) Circles symbolize a python snake, which is highly revered.

(6) The vertical lines stand for the word or the voice.

(7) Symbolically simplified insect

(8) Here we see the dancer in the ritual Kiduma dance.

(9) The symbolic rainbow is of great importance. It was con-
idered a powerful protective deity, for it appeared regularly after
ownpours that were often devastating.

(10) Here we see the symbol for the stars.

(11) This sign shows a crossroad, considered to be a magical
lace by the Congolese.

12) The crocodile, the sacred totem animal, lives at the crossroad.

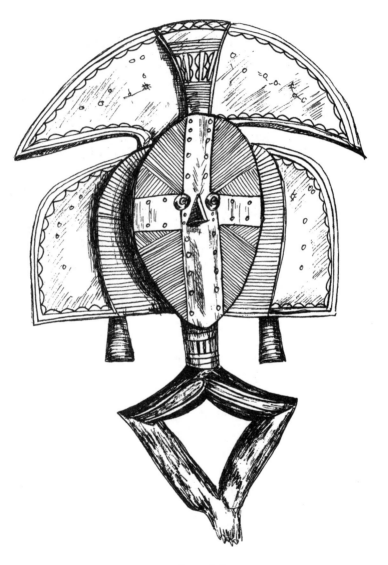

Guard figure

RELIQUARY FIGURE OF THE BAKUBA

Some tribes in Central Africa, the Fang groups, the Kota, and the Mahongwe, follow the custom of keeping the skulls of outstanding members of the clan in relic containers. Usually, these containers are baskets or boxes, which are set with male or female guard figures.

The figure depicted here is from the tribe of the Bakuba who live in the Congo basin. It is a typical example of such a reliquary figure, the primary purpose of which was to prevent the uninitiated from gaining access to the ancestral relics. All these figures display a certain similarity in their external form. They are usually flat, with faces oval and domed either towards the inside or towards the outside. The headdress is arranged in the shape of a lunar crescent and extended on both sides of the face in two rounded surfaces. These wooden figures are partially or completely fitted with copper sheets. The cylindrical neck merges directly into two bent arms, which form the shape of a lozenge. If such a sculpture is mounted on a relic container, it gives the impression of a complete figure.

The guard figure shown here is a female representation, but male figures are equally common. Besides their function as guards of the ancestors, they are also used as puppets. They are carried along during certain dances, and people treat them as representatives of the ancestors.

Magical figure in the shape of a double-headed dog

NAIL FETISH

This double-headed figure comes from the Bakongo in Zaire. Figures like this are called Konde. In their production, they were endowed with magical powers invoked by hammering nails into the sculpture. Over time, this changed the original shape of the fetish.

The double-headed form describes the ability of the spellbound powers to act in both directions, in a beneficial as well as in a detrimental way. For this reason it is difficult for the owner to control them.

The figure gives the impression of power and dangerousness. Because of its ambiguity, it is difficult to determine its purpose. The nails might represent both, a spell with the aim of healing as well as one for doing harm.

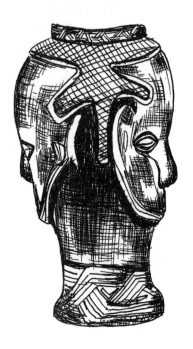

Utensils as symbols of social rank (Zaire)

EVERYDAY ART OF THE KUBA

The Kuba state was located in the area of modern Zaire. Its exclusively male artists are known for their masterly abilities. They created extremely thinly walled containers, which were richly decorated with ornaments.

(1) The double face on this wooden goblet is a portrait of a Nyim (ruler). According to the belief of the Kuba, the spirit of the pictured person enters into the object.

(2) Wooden cup, elaborately decorated with ornaments, from which strong palm wine was drunk. Unfortunately, the meanings of the patterns, which played a role in ritual acts, are no longer known today.

(3) This vessel features ornaments characteristic for the Kuba, such as triangles and intertwined bands. Such vessels were reserved for the upper class. They were status symbols and at the same time utensils of the high dignitaries. The ordinary folk had to be satisfied with less elaborately decorated objects.

Symbol of royal power (Zaire)

WOODEN CUP OF THE KUBA

Among the Kuba, the ram was a symbol of power. For this reason, only kings or great chieftains had the right to drink from a cup such as this. The human head is a portrait of the owner whose spirit animates the vessel. The scar tattoos above the eyebrows and on the cheeks of this dual creature represent a kind of family coat of arms. According to the belief of the Kuba, the spirit of the ruler unites with the spirit of the ram in this object. The cup is a symbol of royal authority and a contributor of magical power.

THE EAST

SUDAN

ETHIOPIA

ERITREA

DJIBOUTI

SOMALIA

UGANDA

KENYA

RWANDA

BURUNDI

TANZANIA

ZAMBIA

MALAWI

MADAGASCAR

1.

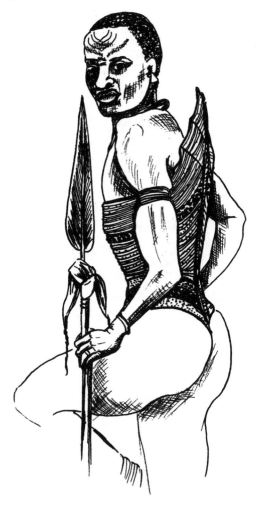

Dinka warrior with skintight pearl corset, Sudan

◆◆

PEARL CLOTHING OF THE DINKA

(1) Dinka warriors go naked except for a skin-tight pearl corset that stays on the body day and night. It consists of many strings of colored pearls that reveal the age group of the men: Red and black pearls for the 15-25 year olds, purple and pink for the 25-30 year olds, and yellow for those over 30. Not until the passage into the next age group is the old corset cut open and exchanged for a new one. The size of the corset says something about the wealth of the person wearing it. The higher the knapsack-like extension on the back, the more livestock the man's family has in its possession. Already a normal-sized corset can have the price of a bull. Sometimes one can also see the women of the Dinka wearing such dress. Their pearl bodice, however, is cut open on the wedding day. Since the Dinka are fond of rounded body shapes, they tie up their upper arms with spirals in such a way that they swell. On the occasion of the ceremonies of passage into adulthood, the young man gets deep, bullhorn-shaped scars cut into his forehead and receives a young bull as a present. The animal gets the same name as the young man and grows up together with him. This often leads to a complete identification, and as a sign of his great affection, the young man decorates the horns of the bull with tassels made from cow tails. Since Dinka men consider it unmanly to cover their bodies, they also sleep naked by the fire. They bleach their hair yellow with a mixture of ashes and the urine of cows.

2.

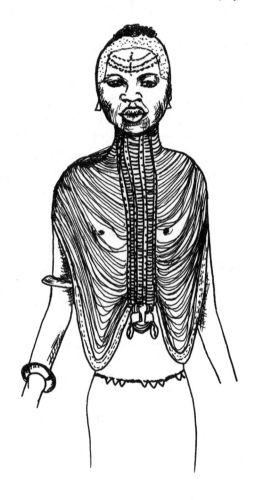

Pearl cape of a marriageable Dinka girl, Sudan

(2) Marriageable Dinka girls display the wealth of their family by means of ornate pearl capes. The integrated cowrie shells are supposed to promote fertility. Except for their ornaments, the girls are likewise completely naked. The triangles on the belt symbolize femininity. Bangles made from several pieces of ivory are usually gifts from admirers and have magical powers. The material itself is a symbol of wealth. The shaved hairline and the ash paste applied in the shape of a helmet only represent a fashion trend. The husband pays the price of the bride in cattle.

1.

3.

2.

Symbolic ornaments of the Massai warriors, Kenya

FESTIVE ORNAMENTS OF THE MASSAI WARRIORS

(1) This drawing shows a Massai warrior during an Eunoto initiation ceremony. For this occasion, he has painted his body with chalk in patterns symbolizing his courage. By means of the lion's mane headdress, he shows that he has killed a lion. The pearl belts, signs of admiration, are presents from the mother and the girlfriends of the young man.

(2) Here we see a headdress made from ostrich feathers as is worn by warriors who have not yet killed a lion. In earlier times, the headdress was supposed to terrify the enemy in war and battle on account of its size. Today, like the lion headdress, it is only worn during dances and ceremonies. To this day, it is the main goal of the young Massai warrior to kill a lion. This increases his popularity among the young women.

(3) Ornamental spirals made from brass are usually worn by the mothers and are awarded to their sons only as part of the Eunoto ceremony. Only those warriors are entitled to them who, on the basis of their character traits, have earned the right to introduce their age group into the class of the elders. During the Eunoto ceremony, the young men get their heads shaven for the first time, indicating their entry into their new life as elders. With this, they earn the right to be heard in the community and to marry. The ceremony signifies the end of the free life as a warrior.

Signs of tribal membership among the Toposa, Sudan

TRIBAL SYMBOLISM OF THE TOPOSA

The pastoral tribe of the Toposa lives in southern Sudan. In order to resemble their revered cattle, many members of the tribe have their lower front teeth pulled out so that the upper jaw protrudes more prominently. As signs of her status, the married woman in the drawing is wearing an iron spiral around her neck, as well as the wedding gift from her husband, a long brass wire in her lower lip, and finally, the typical greased braids. The red seeds at the hairline are lucky charms. The ostrich feather in the hair is a popular status symbol. The ornamental scars and the headband are signs of tribal membership.

Metal spirals, which men and women wear on their forearms, are further symbolic ornaments. Depending on age group and rank (which for men depends on abilities in stealing livestock and in warfare), the Toposa wear arm spirals made of brass, copper, or iron. Here it is important that the arm ornaments of the husband always consist of a different metal than those of his wife.

Motherhood sign of the Rendille, Kenya

ORNAMENTS AND HAIRDRESS OF THE RENDILLE

From the time of the birth of their first son, the women of the Rendille tribe adorn themselves by means of a hair top, which resembles the comb of a rooster. Formed of animal fat, mud, and ocher, this hairstyle is maintained until the boy is circumcised in puberty. Every couple of weeks, the top is carefully restored. Only after the circumcision of the boy or after the death of a close male relative is the head shaven. The iron or brass arm spirals are worn on the forearm during the wedding and on the upper arm after the initiation of the first son.

The Rendille live in the northern desert of Kenya. The neck ornamentation made from doum palm fibers, wrapped with fabric is a popular wedding present. In earlier times, it was made from the hair of an elephant's tail. Samburu women also like to wear these ornaments.

A Rendille woman indicates her fertility by integrating pearls of different colors into her headband.

Ornamental symbols of the Massai, Kenya

STATUS SYMBOLS OF MARRIED MASSAI WOMEN

The oblong pearl ear pendants, which are hooked into the ear-lobes, are a sign that this woman is married. A man must never see his wife without these ornaments. Unmarried girls, by contrast, only wear the kind of delicate ear pendants in the upper part of the ear that can also be seen in the drawing.

Blue pearl necklaces, which are considered divine because of their celestial color, are reserved for married women. The same is true for snuff cases, which, however, are also carried by married men. Green pearls are symbols of peace. They are the "plants after the rain."

The spiral-shaped pendants seen in the picture indicate that the woman has a circumcised son. On the occasion of the recovery period after the circumcision or of the Eunoto initiation ceremony, mothers lend these ornaments to their sons.

Massai women usually shave their heads in order to better accentuate their rich ornamentation. Long hair is reserved for the younger men.

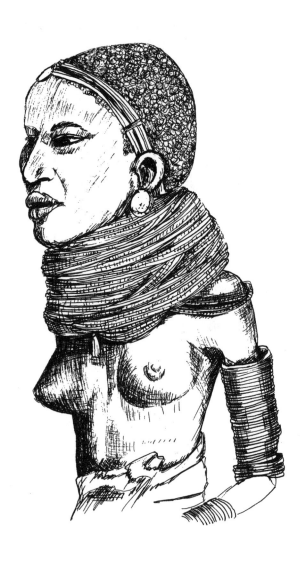

Symbols of social rank (Kenya)

SIGNS INDICATING FAMILY SITUATION

The drawing shows a girl from the tribe of the Tugen in Kenya. Her wire bracelets indicate that her older brother has completed the ceremony of initiation, the glass pearls around her neck and shoulders reveal that she can already have children herself, but that she is not yet married.

A Tugen girl receives these strings of pearls from her admirers. When her chin is pushed up by the number of strings, she is considered beautiful enough to be married.

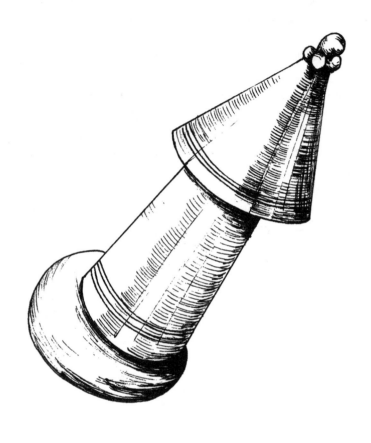

Badge of ritual dignity (Borana & Konso, Ethiopia)

ᵖHALLIC HORN

This horn, a Kalaacha, consists of the materials aluminum and ivory. Among the Konso and the Borana, it is a sacred symbol. Its existence is traced back to the great Kalaacha, the first ritual leader whom God sent to the earth. The horn plays an important role in the Gada system of age and generational relationships.

When a man has reached the Gada stage, he puts on the horn for the first time. It is worn pointing upward on the forehead. It is then said: "The man is making his head." After the completion of this stage, the Kalaacha is kept in a filled container of milk and is worn only during special ceremonies. It may be touched only by its owner and his first wife. During this first Gada stage, the man is ritually responsible for the peace and well-being of the tribe. The second Gada stage is entered when the man leaves his office in order to change into the state of holiness. He prepares for this ceremony by opening his starched shock of hair some time before. He then forms a ring from his hair, in the middle of which the horn is placed. For this age group, the Kalaacha wards off evil and protects the person who touches it.

When leaving the Gada system, the man "takes down his head"; the horn is taken down and the shock of hair is shorn. In some tribal groups, the horns are worn by all members of an age group once everyone in the group has earned a right to one. A precondition of this is the murder of an enemy or of a dangerous animal. In other tribes, the Kalaacha is reserved for special dignitaries. In such cases, one can also find the variant of the double horn.

Grave figure and status symbol of the Konso, Ethiopia

GRAVE FIGURE

If a hero is buried in the tribe of the Konso, a phallic stone is placed on his grave. If a wealthy hero, who belonged to a high Gada tage, dies, then a group of wooden figurines is made some time fter his burial. These figurines describe his feats and achieve-nents. The group is set up on his grave and protected by a thatched oof. The hero himself is one of the middle figures such as is seen n the drawing. He is always represented in an aggressive, mascu-ine pose with an erect penis. His high Gada rank is indicated by the ypical hairdo, the phallic horn, and the numerous bangles. The ther figures, representing his slain enemies, his women, and the easts of prey that he killed, are positioned around him. They usu-lly have no arms, and the male enemies also have no sexual or-ans, since it is customary among the Konso to cut these off as tro-hies. In addition to the figures, rocks are placed on the grave, in-licating the number of fields owned by the deceased.

Similar grave figures are also common among the Bongo in judan and among the Mijikenda in Kenya. The Galla and Borana ribes neighboring the Konso, by contrast, put up carved tomb-tones.

*Carved post which creates the connection to the ancestors
(Mahafaly, Madagascar)*

GRAVE SCULPTURE

Madagascar's most renowned and spectacular ritual objects are the grave posts of the Mahafaly. For the deceased members of its ruling families, this pastoral tribe often constructed giant box-like grave sites, usually from stones left in their natural state. As many thirty carved grave sculptures, usually over two meters high, are then placed onto the platforms of these graves. In the more elaborate pieces, a human figure carries a series of circular and half-moon-shaped symbols representing the lunar phases. Today, moon worship is rare in Africa. And where it is found, it must be regarded more as a relic from the past. Thus, the symbols nowadays also merely serve as ornamental decoration.

These grave sculptures are crowned by an animal representation, usually humpback cattle or birds on their flight home at the end of the day, like the ducks in this drawing. This is supposed to sway the deceased to regard the gravesite as his new home.

The grave posts are called Aloalo, and they are intended to help maintain the connection to the ancestors. The word Alo means mediator. Among the Mahafaly as well, the role of mediator, which the ancestors play vis-à-vis the world of the spirits, is valued highly. For the contact with the deceased makes it possible better to understand and influence the intricacies of life.

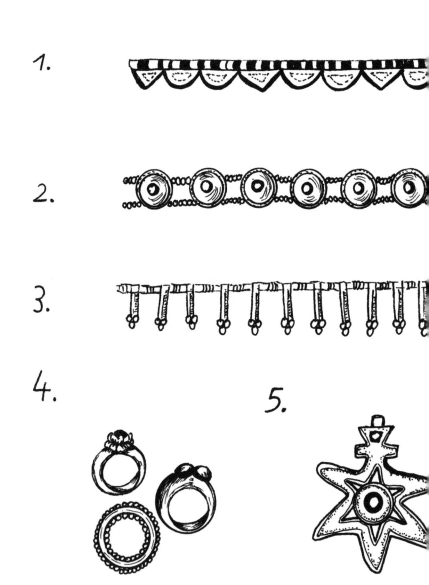

1.

2.

3.

4.

5.

Silver ornaments with Pagan and Jewish symbols (Ethiopia)

YMBOLISM IN THE ORNAMENTS OF THE HIGHLANDS

(1) The triangular pendants of this necklace from Talsum are upposed to protect against the evil eye. In order to reduce the in-luence of the waxing and waning moon, half-moon-shaped pieces vere inserted.

(2) Breast-shaped pearls such as these symbolize fertility. The ame goes for the phallic ornaments in figure (3).

(4) Silver wedding bands such as these are worn on a cotton tring around the neck. They are produced in such a small size that hey are not suited to be worn on the finger.

(5) The Star of David is worn by the Felasha as a sign of their ewish faith.

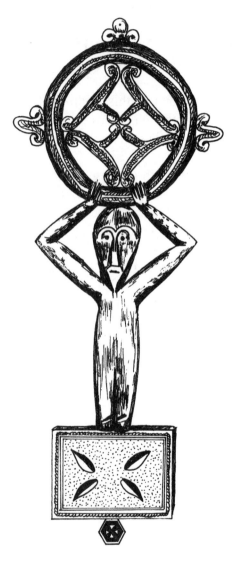

Christian motif describing the creation of mankind (Ethiopia)

HAND CRUCIFIX

By the fourth century, the Ethiopian Empire professed its faith in Christianity and adopted the symbol of the cross as the most important sign of its faith. Large processional crucifixes belong to monasteries and churches, while pilgrims carry pole crucifixes on their shoulders. Hand crucifixes are the property of the priests who let the faithful kiss them and who use them for blessings.

The crucifix shown here shows the cross bearing Adam and at the same time Christ who, as a second Adam, founded a new humanity. The rectangular base refers to Adam's grave on Calvary. Some priests also see in this base slab a reference to the legendary Ark of the Covenant. The handle represents the hope of rebirth, the resurrection from the grave. It also refers to the belief that the cross of Christ was cut from the tree of life.

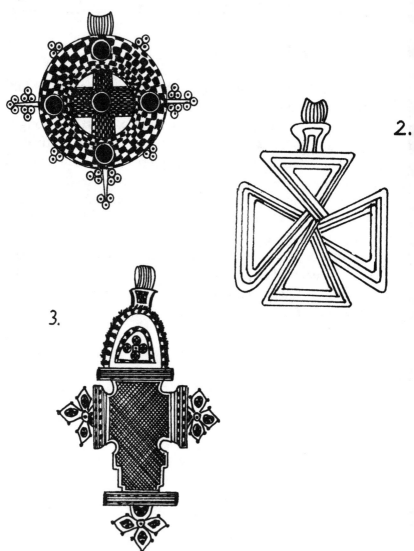

Cross shapes with Christian and universal significance (Ethiopia)

NECK CRUCIFIXES

From the Coptic Christians in Egypt, the Ethiopians adopted the Christian tradition of wearing crucifixes on a blue ribbon around the neck. Besides the usual Latin form, there are also a large number of different designs. The preferred material for these ornaments is silver.

(1) Here we see a crucifix with arms of equal length pointing to the four corners of the world supposedly ruled by the cross. The circle represents the universe, which is also under the sign of the cross. It resembles the so-called Jerusalem crucifix, which has four additional small crucifixes attached between its four arms. The five stones symbolize the wounds of Jesus. The four groups of triple spheres between the outer arms refer to the twelve disciples.

(2) This crucifix with arms of equal length that widen towards the outside belongs to the group of Maltese crosses. The infinite pattern of entwined ribbon points towards eternity.

(3) This is a kind of star crucifix which resembles in its shape the Egyptian Ankh, although the latter is unknown in Ethiopia. The arms of the cross end in three points, thus evoking the trinity. Besides the forms shown here, one also finds the so-called Lotharingian crucifix in Ethiopia. It resembles the Latin crucifix, except that above the main horizontal beam there is yet another ,smaller beam.

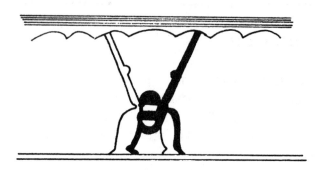

Divine symbols of pre-Christian and Christian Ethiopia

DETAIL OF A FRIEZE

This frieze comes from a temple in Yeha and was later integrated into a church wall. It shows the stylized head of a rock goat. In Saba and Yeha, the god Almaqah was referred to as "god of the rock goats." Such ornaments from ancient Ethiopia are often related to the cultural sphere of Mesopotamia, in the Middle East.

Bulls and rock goats were consecrated to the lunar god Almaqah (also called Sin in some places), who was regarded as the father of the gods. Together with the sun goddess Nuru (also called Zat-Badan), he begot the son Athtar, the Venus god. Besides these, there were a number of other stellar and natural deities.

According to tradition, the queen of Saba is once supposed to have ruled in Yeha. Today, Ethiopia is largely a Christian country where, however, natural spirits and gods are still revered as well.

ROOFTOP CRUCIFIX

This gold-plated crucifix adorns the cathedral in Aksum. In the round churches of Ethiopia, such crucifixes protrude from clay rooftops. They usually feature seven arms. Six of them have been fitted with ostrich eggs as a reminder to the believers to protect their souls from harm, just as the ostrich attentively guards its eggs. In pre-Christian times, there were no crucifixes in Ethiopia, whereas they were already in use as sacred symbols in ancient Egypt and the Orient. The first crucifixes arrived from the Coptic fellow-believers in Egypt in the form of hand crucifixes, which priests and monks carried with them.

Christian representations of saints from Ethiopia

ETHIOPIAN REPRESENTATIONS OF SAINTS

Ethiopian Christianity goes back to early Christianity and the roots of this faith can be traced back to early Judaism. This is why, besides the common saints of the Christian church such as the archangels, typical Ethiopian saints are also revered.

(1) shows a painting of the Ethiopian saint Tekla Haymanot. His portrait, like that of Gabre Manfas Qiddus, can be found in almost every church. Legend has it that Tekla Haymanot once balanced himself on one leg between two spearheads in order to be able to keep the vow of eternal prayer. When the raised leg had died off after seven years, angels took it before God's throne. Thereupon the Lord presented the saint with three pairs of wings.

(2) depicts a mural painting representing Saint Gabre Manfas Qiddus. According to legend, he preached peace to the animals. He moved about the country with lions and leopards, who, on his instruction, ate only grass. He offered the water of his eyes to a thirsty bird.

Also typical for the Christian-Ethiopian art is the representation of Saint George, who, mounted on a white horse, is driving his spear into the throat of a dragon. This picture can be found in every church on the left side of the main door to the sanctuary. The counterpart on the righthand side is usually an image of the Virgin with child.

THE SOUTH

NAMIBIA

BOTSWANA

ZIMBABWE

MOZAMBIQUE

SWAZILAND

LESOTHO

SOUTH AFRICA

Symbol of male maturity (Tsonga, Transvaal)

WOODEN FIGURE FOR INITIATION CEREMONIES

The figure shown here reveals the typical stylistic elements of the Tsonga, the descendants of the Nguni ethnic groups. Characteristic features are the open mouth, the thin arms with spade-shaped hands, clearly marked hips and chest, and the general rod-shaped arrangement. Usually, the figures were used as a pair in order to instruct those to be initiated in social and sexual customs.

Here we have the representation of a man. Curiously, this wooden figure is missing the sexual organs, which are otherwise so prominent in African art.

The headgear of the sculpture represents a head-ring, as was worn by marriageable men. Such a ring consisting of grass and wax was sewn into the scalp of men who had reached the stage of maturity. With this, they gained the right to marriage.

The figure is directly related to the ideas of maturity and masculinity among the Tsonga.

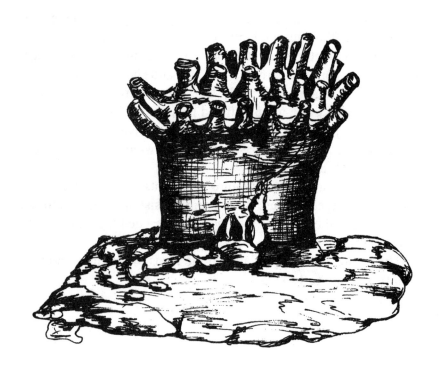

Symbol of power of the rulers (Venda, South Africa)

INGOTS (BARS)

Musuko ingots, such as these, were produced by the tribe of the Venda since the 16th century. They usually consist of copper or tin. The tin bars were primarily used for trading purposes, and thus many of them left the country. Copper bars exist in different forms. Some are hollow and filled with various materials, e.g., granite gravel. Such objects were used in ceremonies.

The size and weight of the ingots varies a great deal and can be anywhere from a few hundred grams to several kilograms. They were formerly cast in sand hollows, with the "spikes" facing down. The meaning of these spikes remains a mystery.

Nowadays, the princes of the Venda revere the few ingots still in their possession as symbols of power and spiritual strength.

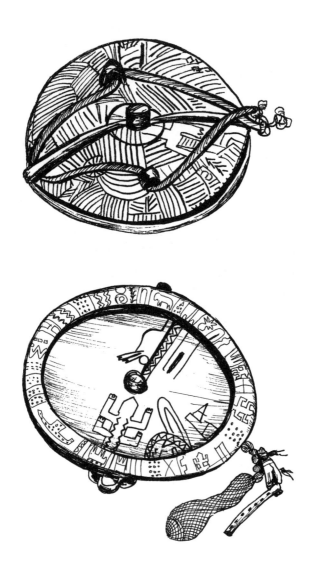

Prophecy instruments decorated with mythical motifs

ORACLE DISH OF THE VENDA

According to legend, the princes of the Venda descend from the legendary hero, Toho ya Ndou, who once led his people from Zimbabwe into the Transvaal. Having founded the capital city, he disappeared into Lake Funduzi, where he holds court underwater.

The interior of the dish is an illustration of this lake kingdom. In the middle, there is an elevation with a cowrie shell. It represents the mountains on which the princes of the Venda founded their settlements. For the purposes of prophecy, the cowrie shell was sprinkled with magic potions. The shell would jut out of the water-filled dish. During consultations, information would be obtained by means of kernels of corn that were thrown into the water. The carved animal motifs represent the various subgroups of the Venda. If the kernels sank, they would be interpreted in accordance with the symbols on which they landed. The crocodile embodies the king, and the fork-like shapes represent his women. The semicircle represents the fence of a pasture. The zigzag line shows the way to the capital, but also represents lightning.

On the outer side of the dish, there are pictorial representations from the worldview of the Venda. The plait pattern refers to the skin of the crocodile, the circles its eyes. The princes of the Venda themselves liked to be referred to as crocodiles. The zigzag motif at the edge represents a python snake that surrounds the shore of the pond in which the crocodile is lying in wait. The python was regarded as a link to the ancestors.

1.

2.

*Utensils which create a link to the ancestors
(Zulu, South Africa)*

UTENSILS WITH SYMBOLIC SIGNIFICANCE

WOODEN MILK BUCKET

(1) In Kwa-Zulu-Natal, such buckets were used for milking. The milk was subsequently transferred into different containers.

The breast-shaped handles are supposed to establish a connection with the female body. Milk was associated with female fertility. The milk buckets always belonged to the male head of the family and were passed on as heirlooms to the male descendants. Women were not allowed to touch them. The vessels represented a symbolic link between the animals and the ancestors of the man.

EARTHEN BEER VESSEL

(2) The Zulus used earthen beer vessels for the transport of sorghum beer. The production of these vessels was reserved for women. The number of attached ornamental studs gave information about the number of livestock on the pasture of the owner. The pattern and arrangement of these studs varied. The ornaments are called Amasumpa. This name refers to the custom of decorating the bodies of young girls with scar tattoos, which formed stud-like protrusions. Among the Zulu, these decorative scars also had a connection to the livestock. The animals not only represented the most important part of the dowry, but also functioned as a link between the ancestors and the living.

Ladle as a symbol of property (Tsonga, Transvaal)

ORNATE LADLE

In many tribes, spoons and ladles, like other African household items, had a special symbolic significance. Usually they were associated in a complex way with the concept of property. They often accompanied their owner to the grave.

The ladle shown here comes from the Tsonga tribe and was used for serving food. It was part of the bridal price that the groom received from the family of the bride at the wedding. In the event of the wife's death, the ladle was given back to her family. Only ornately crafted spoons and ladles had symbolic value.

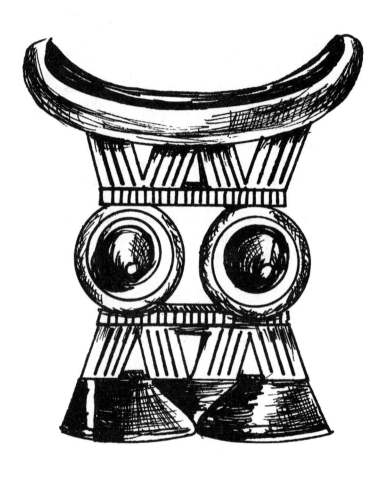

Headrest in the shape of a woman's body (Shona, Zimbabwe)

◆◆

HEADRESTS OF THE SHONA (1)

This wooden headrest comes from the Manyika, a subtribe of the Shona people in the eastern regions of Zimbabwe. It shows the stylized body of a woman without a head. In the middle, there is a clear representation of the breasts. The triangular shapes symbolize the pubic region, the base represents the legs, and the actual resting surface forms the shoulders. In addition, the support is decorated with a stud pattern on the upper surface, which is not visible in the drawing. Such patterns were exclusively tattooed on women in the shoulder, chest, and stomach areas. Among the Shona, the body of a woman, and thus her fertility, were regarded as a loan to the family of her husband, to which, she would never truly belong. Her head, on the other hand, which was seen as the seat of the connection with the ancestral soul, belonged in a certain sense to her father. For this reason, representation of the head is missing from the headrests. Now, if a man uses such a support for sleeping, he complements the object with his head so as to form a complete figure. In this way, he was united with the ancestors. Headrests were used exclusively by married men for the purposes of protecting their complex hairstyles. They received the supports from their wives at the wedding and were buried with them after their death. In some cases, the headrests were also passed on to the descendants. Even today, the priests of the Shona still use such headrests in order to establish a link with the spiritual world.

Headrest with the motif of a crocodile (Shona, Zimbabwe)

HEADRESTS OF THE SHONA (2)

This headrest shows more of a male symbolism, as is common among the Shona people in the South. The two sets of circles represent the eyes of the crocodile, the crossed pattern represent its skin. The crocodile symbolism creates a connection to the tribe of the Venda, which descended from the Shona tribe. The support shows a stylized pond that is associated with the realm of the ancestors. The spirals represent white cone shells that play an important role in the symbolic system of the Shona. There is also a representation of Guano (bird droppings) which was dropped into the pond by fish hawks. White was considered to be the color of spirits. According to the Shona, the fish hawk was in touch with the spiritual world. Hence, special powers are ascribed to his Guano which are made use of by healers and soothsayers.

1.

2.

Symbols of wealth among the Zulu and Nguni, South Africa

HEADRESTS OF THE ZULU AND NGUNI

Wooden headrests were very personal objects of daily use and were often given to accompany their deceased owners into the grave. Depending on the clan, the objects feature specific forms and patterns.

Among the Zulu, the Amasumpa motif seen in illustration (1) was reserved for the members of the royal family. As with other stud like decorations typical of this tribe, the Amasumpa ornaments also refer to the abundance of livestock.

The headrest of the Nguni seen in illustration (2) features the stylized legs and tails of cattle. It is supposed to evoke associations with a great herd. An abundance of livestock was synonymous with wealth. Moreover, the animals provided a means of making contact with the spirits of the ancestors. Cattle were given by the groom as a bridal present. The bride brought the headrests into the marriage as part of her dowry.

SNUFF CONTAINERS

In southern Africa, the consumption of snuff had social significance. It was associated with virility and fertility, which, in turn, signified a connection to the ancestors. Men and women often carried ornate snuff containers as status symbols intended to illustrate wealth, abundance, and the associated generosity. These decorative accessories came in various designs.

1) This little jar was crafted from the horn of a rhinoceros and wood. Thus, it must have been the property of a chieftain, for objects made of ivory of the horn of a rhinoceros were always reserved for the rulers. The material of the container signals fertility. The protruding decorations indicate the wealth of livestock of the owner. The owner of this object was probably a Zulu chieftain.

(2) This container likewise comes from the tribe of the Zulu. It was worn on the arm by means of the double spiral. It is a true masterpiece carved from the horn of an antelope.

On the head of the figure, one can see the outline of a headring, which is an indication of the social rank of

2.

3.

the person wearing it. Hence, the owner had attained the degree of maturity to be able to take on responsibility and establish a family.

Here we see quite an unusual container of the Cape Nguni that consists of animal hide and clay mixed with blood. Standing upright, it resembles a human being. On all fours, however, it also resembles pastoral livestock. The materials probably come from the remains of sacrificial animals that were killed as offerings to the ancestral spirits. Animal-shaped containers create a connection to the spiritual powers of the represented animal species. In Southern Africa, the pastoral livestock is always associated with ancestors, a fact that is also illustrated in this ambiguous figure.

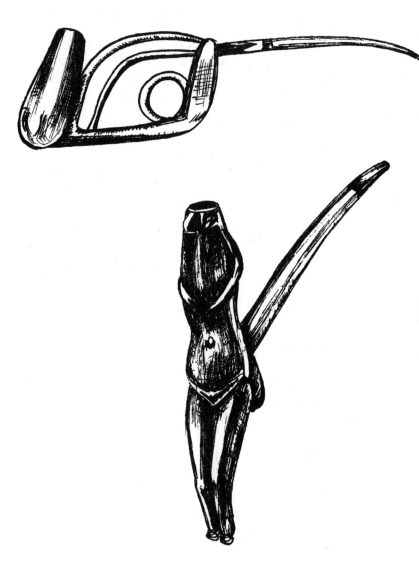

Tobacco pipes as links to the ancestors (South Africa)

TOBACCO PIPES

Smoking was a daily social custom among the Nguni- and Sotho-speaking people in Southern Africa. Tobacco pipes were used by men as well as by women. The size and shape of such a pipe gave information about the social rank and the wealth of its owner. The meanings of the various shapes are no longer known.

The pipes were passed on to the descendants within families, since a connection could be established to the ancestors by means of smoking. The smoke of tobacco made it easier for the spirits to make contact with the material world. Hence, indirectly, the use of tobacco was also connected to fertility and procreation. The pipes connected the present with the past, and tobacco was often a meaningful wedding present.

This beautifully shaped pipe with its curved lines comes from the tribe of the Thembu. The pipe in the shape of a woman's torso is likewise carved from wood and is attributable to the South Sotho tribe.

Door with carved symbol of the chieftain's power (Venda, South Africa)

CARVED WOODEN DOOR OF THE VENDA

Among the Venda, hinged wooden doors were only found in the houses of the ruling families. Doors decorated with reliefs were exclusively reserved for chieftains.

As a whole, the door shown here represents a stylized crocodile: the holes for attaching leather handles are the nostrils; the pegs at the upper and lower end are referred to as teeth; the concentric circles represent the eyes of the crocodile; and the relief-like intertwined pattern is the skin. A similar symbolism is also found on the wooden headrests of the Venda.

The crocodile was seen as the equal of the political and spiritual power of the chieftain. The ruler himself was referred to as the crocodile in the pond. During their inauguration, the chieftains used to swallow stones taken from the stomachs of crocodiles. They kept them in their bodies until death. In many ruling houses, stuffed crocodiles were used as pillows.

If the wooden door was closed, one would say, "the crocodile is biting." If it was open, one would say, "the crocodile is letting go."

Today, doors of this kind are no longer in use among the Venda. But old wooden doors are still used in the initiation ceremonies for young girls.

1.

2.

Representations from the world of stories of the San, South Africa

DECORATED OSTRICH EGGS

The San used ostrich eggs as drinking cups or as containers for storing make-up powder or ant larvae (bushman's rice). Ostrich eggs filled with water and sealed were also buried in hidden places in the sand in order to ensure a water supply.

The decorations etched into the eggs are not nearly as rich in symbolism as the rock paintings of the San, although they are likewise connected to mythology. In the first place, the engravings provide a reference to the person who produced them. Since the concept of property does not exist in the minds of the bushmen, the objects were used by the entire group.

(1) The engraving on this ostrich egg shows a stylized Elen antelope, which plays a central role in the worldview of the San. Like the groups of the San, the Elen antelopes seasonally unite into larger herds and later split again into smaller groups. Hence, the bushmen identify in a certain way with the Elen antelopes. In their eyes, these animals are the main carriers of spiritual power.

(2) This drinking vessel is decorated with snake motifs. The snake is considered the mediator between life and death. Among the San, the snake plays a central role in the entry into the trance, an experience, that is equated with a death experience, since it also constitutes an entry into the world of spirits.

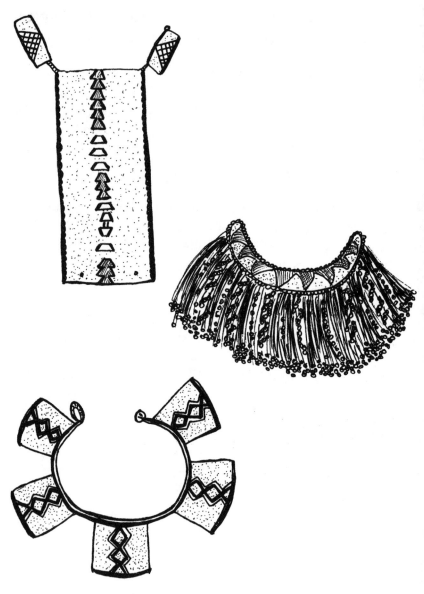

Neck pendant, loincloth, and "speaking necklace" of the Zulu, South Africa

ZULU ORNAMENTS

(1) Long neck pendant of the Zulu tribe, which was supposed to protect the person wearing it from evil spirits. The background is made of white pearls, while the ornaments are red, blue, and black. The red color points to the power and strength of the blood; the blue triangles pointing upward represent defense.

(2) This drawing shows a loincloth of the kind worn by young unmarried Zulu girls. It is made of leather and strings of pearls. The embroidered triangles stand for femininity.

(3) Tiny love letters in the shape of a necklace are made by Zulu girls and presented to the young men of the tribe. The shape and color transmit messages to the recipient such as love, disappointment, hope, or the call to begin courting. Pink pearls stand for poverty. Green signals coolness; white indicates a pure heart and loneliness. Royal-blue pearls spell rejection: "You are a croaking, straying bird." Black says: "Darkness prevents me from coming to you." The drawing shows the characteristic form of the "speaking Zulu necklaces."

Distinguishing marks of married women of the Pondo and Ndebele tribes, South Africa

HAIR CIRCLET EMBROIDERED WITH PEARLS

(1) The decoration on this embroidered circlet points to the fact that the woman wearing it is married. The Pondo women indicate the stages of their lives by wearing hair circlets bearing the corresponding symbols. Countless white pearls form the background for the colored ornaments.

LOINCLOTH EMBROIDERED WITH PEARLS (MA-PATO)

(2) A loincloth such as this is made either of embroidered goatskin, like the one shown here, or is made of linen. They are worn by the married women of the Ndebele as a sign of their status. The ornament in the middle is a popular pattern for dances and festivities. The traditional white background color is animated with blue and red patterns.

In contrast to west and central Africa, in the southern part of the continent, pearls and pearl-embroidered dress were accessible to the whole population and almost had the character of a national costume. Among the Bantu tribes of South Africa, objects decorated with pearls are used on a daily basis. They usually give information about the social status, the stage of life, or the marital status of the person wearing them.

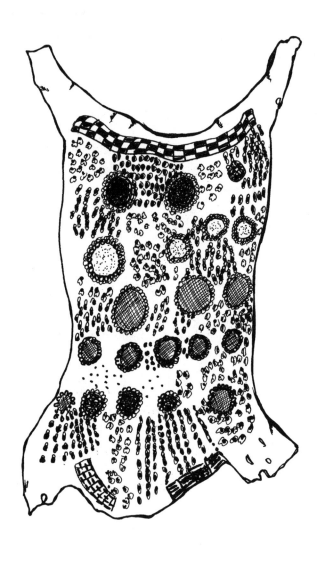

Magical garment for the protection of unborn life (Nguni, South Africa)

◆◆◆

LEATHER APRON EMBROIDERED WITH PEARLS

This maternity apron of the Nguni was worn for the protection of the unborn child. After the birth of the child, the leather skins were often used as carrying cloths.

Traditionally, the loincloth was made from the skin of an animal, which had been sacrificed to the ancestors of the father in order to ensure good luck and health in the life of the child. The animal form of the skin was preserved in order to emphasize the relation to the ancestors. The collar and the tie strings are formed by the hind legs. As far as we know, the various pearl ornaments do not contain any particular messages. Only the large number of pearls reveals the high social rank of the owner of the apron.

Today, the traditional animal skin garments of South Africa are often replaced by imported cloth garments. Yet maternity aprons are still made from animal skin because of the deep symbolic meaning.

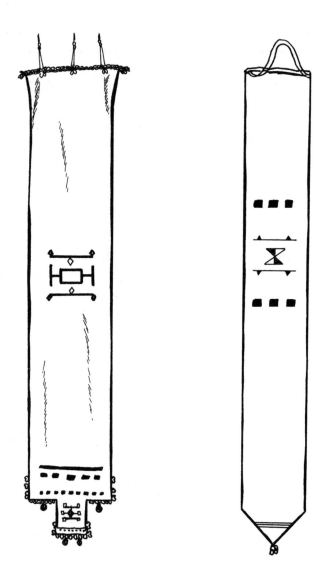

Pearl-embroidered trails of the Ndebele women, South Africa

◆◆

NYOKA

Traditionally, the Ndebele women wear such pearl-embroidered trails as an indication of their social status. These trails are either tied to the head by means of a ribbon or sewn to the back of cloaks made from animal hide. In earlier times, many women would wear two trails at once-one on the back and another at the front. Nyokas were originally worn on a daily basis, while nowadays they are reserved only for special occasions such as weddings, initiations, or funerals.

The trails are completely embroidered with white pearls. The white color is associated with social change and a change of consciousness. Nothing is known anymore about the meanings of the sparingly used colored motifs. Nowadays, these patterns are rather subject to fashion. During the transition through the various stages of maturity, the old embroidered patterns are partially unraveled and then newly arranged under the supervision of the older women.

The term Nyoka means snake. This suggests a connection to the ancestors and to fertility.

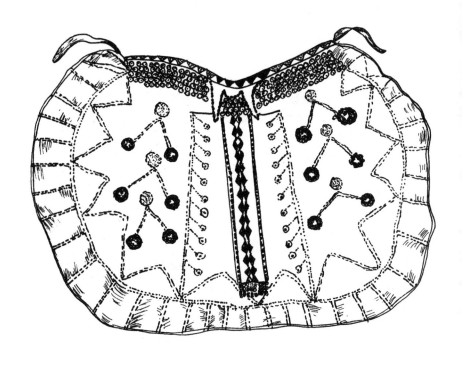

Sign of social position among the Ndebele, South Africa

NDEBELE CAPE DECORATED WITH PEARLS

The characteristic capes of the Ndebele tribe consisted of sheepskins, which were sewn in the typical semicircular shape. A young woman would receive the cape at the occasion of her wedding from her father. The pearl decorations and pearl pendants were only gradually added later and could turn out quite variously.

The wearing of these precious capes was always connected with the transition to a new social position. It revealed the new status of the bride, or it told of a proud mother, if it was worn by the son after graduation from the initiation school, and it assured older women the respect they deserved because of their age.Today, woolen fabrics are usually used instead of skins.

Cave drawing of the trance travels of a shaman (San, South Africa)

ROCK PAINTING OF THE SAN (BUSHMEN)

This drawing shows a detail from the Linton slab, which was found in a cave in the Drakensberg massif. It shows the trance experiences of a shaman and a wealth of religious motifs. The large figure lying down represents a shaman whose arms have transformed into animal legs with hooves. He is connected with the other creatures in the picture by means of a red line. It symbolizes his spiritual travels in a state of trance. In this state, it was possible for the shaman to influence the weather and the animals or to heal the sick. During his bodiless travels, he would often assume the shape of an animal. In the worldview of the San, the main carrier of this power is the antelope. In the illustration, the antelope touches one of the legs of the shaman, opening the way for him into the realm of spirits. While this is happening, the antelope is bleeding from the nose, like a person in a state of trance. In the picture on the left there is another reference to the death-like experience of the shaman. The shape of a snake with the head of an antelope is bleeding from the nose, demonstrating the experience of death. The visions of the shaman are also represented in various ways in the picture. On left, the head of an antelope is protruding from a colored circle. The eels below the body of the shaman describe the underwater experience of the trance. As in the case of someone drowning, one is struggling for air and there is a sense of lightness and a dimming of consciousness.

The creation of such rock paintings was supposed to prompt the spirits hiding behind rocks to join the world of humans.

1.

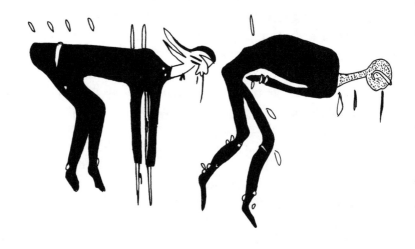

Trance dance of the San

MURAL PAINTINGS OF THE SAN (1)

Here we see two trance dancers of the San people. The left dancer is wearing a wrap made of antelope skin, the head of which was pulled over in such a way that the ears are sticking out like they would on an animal. The head of the right dancer is decorated by a cap with two long feathers. The folded posture of the figures is typical of the trance dance: it is brought about by a sensation which medicine men describe as "cooking." As soon as the dancers sense the rise of the energy along the spine, they are seized by a quiver that makes it impossible to stand up straight. They then support themselves by means of the dance sticks, like the man on the left. At the climax of the trance, both begin to bleed from their noses. The blood or its smell is used to heal the sick. The trance dancers stand in direct connection to the dying Elen antelope, which is likewise bleeding from the nose. In their state, the dancers unite with the spiritual power of the animals and thus gain the power of healing. According to the San, the trance is a deathlike state.

Cave drawing of a healing ceremony

MURAL PAINTINGS OF THE SAN (2)

This rock painting shows a healing ceremony in which trance dancers, who have appropriated the supernatural powers of the Elen antelopes, are walking around the sick person. They put their hand on him or grab him under the shoulders. Similar ceremonies are still taking place today. The women form a protective circle around the group. In the event that one of the dancers is overcome by the spiritual power, falls to the ground, and leaves his body, the women will look after him. In such a case, they will hold an herb under his nose which diminishes the effect of the trance. They will wipe the sweat off his body and dance and sing around him until he awakens again.

INDEX

318